Praise for

MY SON AND
THE AFTERLIFE

"Elisa's journey has been amazing, and she is well-qualified to
share her knowledge with both the medical community and the grief
community. She has the credentials to bridge the gap that often exists
between these two groups, and by doing so, she is breaking new
ground and leading the way for many of us working in the field
of bereavement, hospice care, and consciousness."

—**Terri Daniel**, author, educator, end-of-life adviser,
interfaith chaplaincy, and founder/director of the
Afterlife Education Foundation and
the Annual Afterlife Awareness Conference

"*My Son and the Afterlife* contains the clearest, most
informative answers to questions about what happens after a
person passes into the afterlife that I have read in one book.
The topics explored range from very human, personal issues such
as who greets the person after their passing to insightful descriptions
of the nature of consciousness and reality."

—**R. Craig Hogan, PhD**, author of *Your Eternal Self*

"Erik's messages are poignant, profound, informative, and entertaining, and above all, give us that assurance that we all long for—that there is life beyond death and that all is well there. Erik's words help our minds to understand, but most of all, he helps our hearts to heal and our joy to soar. Thank you, Erik."

—**Christine Elder**, author of *Broken Blessings*

"*My Son and the Afterlife* is a book that will tug at your heartstrings, and make you laugh, cry, and more importantly, consider possibilities that you have probably never thought about before. This book, a record of the author's conversations with her deceased son Erik, is as real, authentic, and straightforward as it gets. Dr. Medhus and her son Erik are both in a state of flux, struggling to make sense of new perspectives that were thrust upon them as a result of Erik's suicide. Both are determined to fully explore and share their newfound awareness as they provide much-needed healing for each other, find new meaning and significance in the love that binds them, and invite you to come along on their poignant journey to the other side of death."

—**Thomas Campbell**, physicist and author of *My Big TOE (Theory of Everything)*

"Raised by atheist parents, Elisa Medhus, MD, believed only in a material reality—until her mind was jarred open by the excruciating loss of her son Erik. Following his death, she began to receive anomalous communications matching Erik's distinctive personality. Always direct and sometimes crude, the insightful messages forever changed Elisa's worldview. I was touched by the continuing dialog between mother and son, finding it both comforting and enlightening. Don't be surprised if Elisa's story alters your ideas about the nature of reality too."

—**Mark Ireland**, author of *Soul Shift*

"The hidebound reductionist materialism of nineteenth- and early-twentieth-century science is crumbling under new discoveries and their relevance to what sensitive people through the ages have known all along. Dr. Medhus meticulously guides us through her own epiphany as she, a medical doctor, an exploring mind, and a suddenly refocused mother, finds the intensely personal strength to understand her son's suicide and its larger meaning in the Nature of which we are all part, and the courageous professional strength to bring her realizations to us.

"While this book is obviously an invaluable resource for theologians and physicists, and ethicists and counselors, it is truly a touchstone for all of us who feel and who seek to understand the transcendental nature of the human condition."

—Marco M. Pardi, MA, DPS, anthropologist and thanatologist

"Dr. Elisa Medhus has approached her conversations with her son Erik in a courageous and systematic way, using all the analytical skills of a trained scientist. She asks Erik the hard questions that any parent who has lost a child would want answers to and more. Erik answers all these questions with his own characteristic laid-back directness in a no-nonsense way that brings our understanding of the afterlife into the twenty-first century. This is a remarkable book written by remarkable people, which will bring hope and comfort to the bereaved and change many lives for the better."

—Dr. Victor Zammit, author of
A Lawyer Presents the Evidence for the Afterlife

MY SON AND THE AFTERLIFE

MY SON AND THE AFTERLIFE

CONVERSATIONS FROM THE OTHER SIDE

ELISA MEDHUS, MD

ATRIA PAPERBACK
New York London Toronto Sydney New Delhi

BEYOND WORDS
Hillsboro, Oregon

ATRIA PAPERBACK
A Division of Simon & Schuster, Inc.
1230 Avenue of the Americas
New York, NY 10020

BEYOND WORDS
20827 N.W. Cornell Road, Suite 500
Hillsboro, Oregon 97124-9808
503-531-8700 / 503-531-8773 fax
www.beyondword.com

Managing editor: Lindsay S. Brown
Editors: Emily Han and Sylvia Spratt
Copyeditor: Sheila Ashdown
Proofreader: Jennifer Weaver-Neist
Design: Devon Smith
Composition: William H. Brunson Typography Services

First Atria Paperback/Beyond Words trade paperback edition October 2013

ATRIA PAPERBACK and colophon are trademarks of Simon & Schuster, Inc. Beyond Words Publishing is an imprint of Simon & Schuster, Inc. and the Beyond Words logo is a registered trademark of Beyond Words Publishing, Inc.

For more information about special discounts for bulk purchases, please contact Simon & Schuster Special Sales at 1-866-506-1949 or business@simonandschuster.com.

The Simon & Schuster Speakers Bureau can bring authors to your live event. For more information or to book an event, contact the Simon & Schuster Speakers Bureau at 1-866-248-3049 or visit our website at www.simonspeakers.com.

Manufactured in the United States of America

10 9 8 7 6 5 4 3 2

Library of Congress Cataloging-in-Publication Data

Medhus, Elisa.
    My son and the afterlife : answers from the other side / Elisa Medhus, MD. —
1st Atria paperback/Beyond Words trade paperback ed.
        pages   cm
1. Science and spiritualism.   I. Title.
BF1275.S3M43   2013
133.9'1—dc23

                                                                    2013014956

ISBN 978-1-58270-461-6
ISBN 978-1-4767-4471-1 (ebook)

The corporate mission of Beyond Words Publishing, Inc.: *Inspire to Integrity*

To my husband, Rune Medhus—the steadfast rock and loving arms I needed in my darkest moments of grief

CONTENTS

PART II: THE UNTETHERED SOUL

PART III: THE BIGGER PICTURE

FOREWORD

by ERIK MEDHUS
(AS TRANSLATED BY JAMIE BUTLER)

My life has never really been what I would consider ordinary. I now have an extraordinary life in the afterlife, and I find myself explaining and sharing my journey.

I did not have a life's path on Earth, but now I am grateful to say I define myself by the work I do. Despite all the pain and suffering our family has gone through, I know in my soul, my death was timely. It triggered my scientifically minded mother to research grief and death. It led her to ask questions and to discover how to continue a relationship with her deceased son. In the middle of all this, she ended up giving us both a voice with which to help others learn about death, the afterlife, suicide, grief, and communication.

I could not have done this without my mother. Mom, I love you so much. Thank you for not giving up on me, even through death. Love does triumph over all.

I also want to tell my family "thank you." I love you more than you know. I am with you every step of the way.

FOREWORD

by JAMIE BUTLER
(ERIK'S SPIRIT TRANSLATOR)

In the summer of 2010, I had my first scheduled appointment with Elisa Medhus. I sat upstairs in my parents' home in Florida, seeking privacy. The only prior knowledge I had was her name and phone number. After Elisa phoned in, the spirit of a young man came into the room. He looked to be about eighteen years old and was tall and thin. His hair was a little unkempt. When he chose to look my way, his eyes gazed right through me; but most of the time, his eyes darted around the room, or he hung his head a bit, looking down at the floor. He was unsettled. He was dressed in jeans and a T-shirt, and he told me that he was the caller's son.

He started to talk about his passing—spirits often do this. I find it not only helps the people left behind to hear validation of what their loved one went through, but it helps the spirit to talk through it too. Elisa told me his name was Erik. He then began to explain that he took his own life. I recall hesitating several times through the story, as it was painful for me, as a mother, to listen and translate. Elisa took the information in stride and with such love. I was impressed with and in awe of her strength.

Erik continued, and as soon as he became comfortable with me, he began throwing in some "sailor talk." I stuttered over the coarse words and giggled nervously, trying to keep pace with this young man's sassiness. Elisa paused and assured me that, if this was her Erik, this was the language she expected. She encouraged me to accept him, as well as his choice of language. This is how I came to know Erik.

Becoming Erik's communicator and translator has been incredibly challenging, humbling, and enlightening. Watching him grow into his new shoes, and teach with compassion and his trademark brashness, has pushed me to think beyond the limits of spirituality. I am so grateful to be a part of Erik's spiritual family.

I have been talking with spirits my entire life and often find more comfort in them than in my earthly friends. For me, death is a beautiful rebirth, a return to our essence. Death is not an ending but a new beginning. And teaching this perspective is one of the most significant aspects of my work.

My beliefs are nothing new, but the process of understanding and incorporating these beliefs into our daily lives—this is what is new to us. My intention is to translate the messages from Erik and other wonderful spirit guides, making the information digestible, understandable, and useable. I hope that this will be your experience.

INTRODUCTION

As a mother, I find it painful to watch my children struggle. As a physician, this pain is compounded by the fact that I couldn't "fix" my son Erik, who struggled daily with demons that tormented him mercilessly. Along with learning difficulties and Tourette's syndrome, he also suffered from severe bipolar disorder, a vicious monster that carried him into the darkest, deepest caves from which he eventually never surfaced.

Bipolar disorder can be a terminal disease, and in Erik's case, it was. One beautiful autumn day, I found him dead, sitting in his chair after putting a .45-caliber, hollow-point bullet through his brain. At that point, my life changed from the "before" to the "after." I plunged not only into grief and despair but also into a vacuum devoid of any belief system that would answer what would become the most important question of my life: Where is my son? As a physician with a strong science background, who was raised by two atheists, I found it difficult to know where to start my search. I didn't even know whether there was anything to search *for*.

So, I did what I do best: I turned to science. I devoured hundreds of books and accounts by quantum and theoretical physicists and near-death experiencers. I reviewed controlled, double-blind experiments conducted on spiritual translators, and I explored scientific studies on the survival of consciousness after death. Even before Erik died, I always wondered: *Is there more to life than what is contained in the limited, three-dimensional reality we perceive with our five senses?* If we limit our beliefs to those ingrained in us by the material sciences and by most organized religions, we are left with so many unexplained phenomena. Why are some spirit translators uncannily accurate? Why do some children recount such compelling past-life stories? Why are some near-death experiences so hard to dismiss as delusional? Because of my strong science background, I always felt at odds with spiritual matters, but I was also familiar with the principle of Occam's razor: The most plausible answer is that which explains the most and assumes the least. For me, to believe in the survival of consciousness after death honored this concept. Maybe the world wasn't flat after all.

Why are people like me so skeptical about the spiritual and the paranormal? We are skeptical because we label something as "real" only when we can observe it directly with our senses or with a measuring device that delivers the information to our senses. Thomas Campbell, experimental nuclear physicist and author of *My Big TOE* (Theory of Everything), explains that we are like our intestinal bacteria. For all we know, the bread that comes down to us is manna from Heaven. We know nothing of the sowing of the seeds, the irrigation, the crop rotation, the fertilization and pest control, the harvesting, the production of bread and its transportation to market. But it still affects us, the bacteria.[1] That said, there is much out there that exists and affects us all even though we cannot perceive it with our senses. Other dimensions, including the one my son is in, may be one such thing. But a big ship changes its course very slowly, and as the philosopher Arthur Schopenhauer is often said to have observed, "All truth passes through three stages. First, it is ridiculed. Second, it is violently opposed. Third, it is accepted as being self-evident."[2]

As an open-minded skeptic now equipped with scientific studies—including research on spirit translators—that supported my hypothesis,

I began my search for a gifted translator who could give voice to my son. I found exactly what I set out to find in Jamie Butler. In our sessions, she perfectly captured Erik's irreverent personality, and the chemistry between the two was clearly special, like an older sister and her pestering little brother.

With the information from those sessions, I began my blog, *Channeling Erik: Conversations with My Son in the Afterlife*. At first, the blog was a way to vent my grief, as well as a way to continue a relationship with my son. But as the membership grew, I was amazed by how many people found solace in my daily posts. For some, the blog was lifesaving. Literally.

Eventually, the blog members and I began to ask Erik questions, and those answers provided us with comfort and hope. Throughout this book, Erik describes the death process, the nature of the afterlife, the abilities and activities of an untethered soul, the fate of suicides, and the meaning of life and the human experience, as well as other matters. On the subject of suicide, Erik adamantly makes a case against it. Over and over again, he says that when you take your life, your troubles don't end; you take them with you. Furthermore, you leave a world of grief in your wake, which only compounds your pain. How well I can attest to that.

Erik would be the first to admit that he is no Oracle of Delphi. He's an imperfect human being who, like many of us, has battled his own dragons. He has stumbled and failed over and over. But perhaps because of his foibles, he has a deep understanding of the human experience. He knows what it's like to be neck-deep in a foxhole of misery, clawing to pull himself out. He also knows what it's like to feel hopelessness and give up, believing that life is not worth the pain and setbacks. But these trials and tribulations offer another type of wisdom—one many of us can relate to in the shadow of our own hardships. That said, however young and imperfect, Erik has a voice worth hearing. He is one of us.

As a physician, writing this book has been a healing experience for me: it is in my nature to heal, and by helping others, I heal my own wounds as well. As a mother, writing this book has taught me an important lesson: death does not mean the end of a relationship. Love knows no boundaries—not even death.

I invite you to join Erik and me on this journey. Consider this book a guide to the afterlife—a handbook of sorts, in which you can refer to specific chapters time and time again, as needed. At times you will cry. At times you will laugh. At times you will pause in wonderment. Some of you are bereaved like me. Some of you wish to overcome a fear of death. Some of you yearn to see the bigger picture, to grasp the meaning of life and death.

Whatever your motives, together we will explore the meaning of the human experience, the nature of the death process, the proof and architecture of the afterlife, the survival of the soul and consciousness, and the physics behind it all. Like me, many of you will begin this journey as skeptics. It is my hope that we will end that journey together in peaceful enlightenment.

How This Book Works

A large part of my journey from skeptic to believer required answers from the "other side"—conversations with someone who, at first, I wasn't sure even existed: my son. Much of this book is comprised of transcripts of these conversations with Erik, which were facilitated by his spiritual communicators and translators, Jamie Butler and Kim O'Neill. On that subject, "forewarned is forearmed," as they say, so I'd like to mention that, in these conversations, Erik is very much himself, including a bit of classic Erik "sailor talk," so please be aware that you will encounter some at-times colorful language as he speaks his mind.

That said, I invite you to listen in while Erik, Jamie, Kim, and I (referred to as "Me" in the transcripts) engage in dialogue that is informative, occasionally irreverent and challenging, often intimate, sometimes heartbreaking, and always illuminating. I encourage you to use this book as you see fit: as a reference for skipping around to particularly relevant sections or points of interest, or as a traditional cover-to-cover reading experience. My goal is for you to find a complete guide to death and the afterlife in between the front and back covers of this book—a compendium of information to which you can refer over and over again.

The Skeptical Mind: My Journey to Belief

Being raised by two atheists was, in many ways, like housing the mind in an iron box with no windows or doors. It did have its advantages. I didn't have to think or question; my mind was closed to the two-way flow of all ideas related to life after death. On the other hand, it left me with no tools with which to explore that subject.

Throughout my life, I have encountered many examples of the existence of life after death, but my doubts have tested the sturdiness of my iron box. For example, I stumbled upon a television show covering the many uncanny visions and predictions of Edgar Cayce, American spirit translator and founder of the Association for Research and Enlightenment. I read a fascinating *New York Times* article about toddler twins found inexplicably speaking the ancient language of Aramaic. I encountered a news report about a Seattle woman who had a near-death experience following a heart attack. While allegedly in an out-of-body state, the woman noticed a tennis shoe, with the laces folded underneath the heel, stuck on a ledge of the hospital's third floor. The exact shoe was later retrieved by hospital staff, from the exact location the woman specified.

Although I couldn't explain the uncanny accuracy of some spiritual communicators' predictions, the seemingly indisputable accounts of near-death experiencers, and the extraordinary past-life stories told by children, I remained stubbornly close-minded. And because of that bias, I harbored insensitive thoughts toward others. For example, whenever people spoke of energy healing, past-life regression, or spirit communication, I dismissed them as New Age, airy-fairy kooks, or I envisioned gypsies hunched over crystal balls. Also, the close-minded lifestyle I led sometimes caused me pain. For example, my father's first words to me after Erik died were, "I'm sorry, Elisa, but he's going to turn to dust." Oh, how I wanted to believe he was wrong.

I have been an internist, certified by the American Board of Internal Medicine, for over half of my life, with decades devoted to a private practice. Biology, biochemistry, pharmacology, pathology, physiology, and other branches of the sciences are practically a part of my DNA. In fact, science is squeezed so tightly between those double helices that I thought there was no room for what I once considered "nonsense." This point of view only served to further reinforce that iron box of skepticism. Again, the fact that I couldn't perceive my deceased son with any of my senses challenged everything I had learned throughout my education. How could I possibly redefine my entire identity as a scientist, a doctor, and a skeptic?

But after Erik died, he started to present himself to family and friends. Erik visited them in vivid, profound dreams and even started to play mischievous pranks. It seemed like almost everyone was enjoying his presence but me. I felt jealous, because, after all, I was his mother. I could have dismissed them as completely deluded, but I knew these people weren't crazy, especially not my husband. He's as rational and sane as they come. These experiences, coupled with my exhaustive research, marked the beginning of my internal tug-of-war between wary skepticism and belief.

I have always been critical of physicians who make up their minds about a patient's diagnosis after reading his or her chart, even before the interview or examination. I pride myself on keeping an open mind while listening to my patients and tapping in to my own intuition. As I began to question my skepticism surrounding the concept of life after death, I asked myself: *Do I really want to be one of those people who insists that the Earth is flat?* Still, I refused to acquiesce. I clung to my disbelief like a tenacious bulldog, because to believe, only to then be proven wrong, would be to lose Erik all over again. I just couldn't bear that.

As my grief began to lift ever so slightly, I finally started to receive visits and pranks from Erik. Later, I learned that profound grief is a dense wall that makes communication with the deceased difficult, if not impossible. This is how my journey from close-mindedness to cautious, open-minded skepticism began, and all it took was a bit of faith. Now my iron box has windows and doors. That said, everyone has a vested interest in whether there is something more after death, but close-minded skeptics, like the former me, are oftentimes too afraid to trust the research, their intuition, or any shred of evidence. If they were to find out the truth, it would require a paradigm shift of massive proportions. I know. I've done it. It takes courage and strength to trust, to have faith, and to be completely open. Now, at last, I have these things. The purpose of this journey is to share what I have found along the way with those who may be traveling down a similar path.

From Erik: A Case Against Suicide

Through my death, I have learned that you can't look at one answer for life's many questions and assume that it's going to fit everyone. Even things that we consider to be pretty constant, like time, aren't. What I have gathered about life is that we as people are gathering together in difficult circumstances to relearn what love is. Love of the self; of others; of our surroundings; of animals, plants, and inanimate items—the list goes on. All things on Earth can be loved and can receive love.

When we are learning about love, we learn to place no judgment; we learn to be resilient and let the pain of life and others move through us; and we learn to accept life as it is without forcing shit to happen. We are very much in control of what we can be; the rest is a strong yet delicate fabric of energy that weaves us around each other. If we choose to ignore this energy, it will be the one thing that suffocates us.

I will not stand and condone suicide, nor will I be the guy who tells you that suicide is for the weak. I will not say suicide is honorable either. I will say that suicide is a way out of life. It is a self-expression—one that is very clear. It says, "I am done." Suicide is a personal choice, and it's not up to you to judge the person who chooses it. We are all looking for love, not judgment. In retrospect, I see that the struggle of life on Earth has powerful meaning. I would encourage those who are considering suicide, or who have thought of suicide as a choice, to set it aside. Try your hand at being loved. The ultimate goal is to live out your life and experience love on Earth. All we can do is our personal best. Don't limit yourself.

PART I

ERIK'S LIFE, DEATH, AND AFTERLIFE

1

ABOUT ERIK

Erik was born on September 21, 1989, at three in the afternoon. He greeted the world without even a whimper. Instead of howls of protest at the bright lights and cool air, he seemed content to take in his surroundings peacefully. Until he was around twelve or thirteen, he was a happy boy.

As a child, Erik had a keen eye for beauty. He adored women and was not afraid to compliment them on their hair or eyes or clothes, and he even proposed marriage to several female teachers in preschool. Whenever he went on walks with his classmates, he would stop to admire every flower, every insect, and every weed—much to the dismay of his teachers. Erik also adored all things macho. He loved military garb and paraphernalia. He loved motorcycles, motocross—motor-anything. He enjoyed working on engines, fixing his friends' cars, and installing stereo systems and lift kits for them. Erik was also quite the clotheshorse. He loved dressing up in "Pappa suits" (a name that Erik coined as a kid for business suits), and, in the months before his death, he often walked around in a suit and tie for no reason at all. He was truly a man's man.

In keeping with his penchant for masculine endeavors, Erik longed to participate in all the sports his father engaged in: motorcycle racing, motocross, slalom skiing, and other activities that caused me as a mother and wife to close my eyes and cringe. But he was clumsy like me, and my husband, Rune, is a very protective father, so Erik never did get to participate in those death-defying endeavors to the extent that he wanted. I think his clumsiness is a sign that, like me, Erik is more comfortable in spirit than in the physical.

As masculine as Erik was, he was also a sensitive boy. He instinctively knew when people needed a hug or a kind word of encouragement. Even as young as nine months old, he would pat our backs to comfort us when we held him in our arms to provide him with comfort! Erik never wanted to upset anyone. I remember one day, when he was around two or three years old, I brought him home from the pediatrician's office, thighs and arms littered with Band-Aids from immunizations. It had been a tough afternoon for the little guy. But when his father asked how he was, Erik answered with a smile on his tear-stained face: "I have a good time."

As he grew up, Erik's charm and charisma only blossomed more. His smile and laugh could light up a room. He never knew a stranger and would talk the ear off of anyone he met. As much as he could talk about his life, though, he was even better at asking others about theirs. Erik was a master at listening to others with great patience and compassion. He also reached out to those he felt were struggling like him. I can't begin to count the number of "strays" he brought home for Mama's cooking and for the nurturing companionship of our family. Erik's sense of play was infectious; he loved being silly, playing pranks, and crafting wonderful jokes for all to enjoy. None of his jokes or pranks were mean spirited—they were all loving and endearing.

Erik had noble priorities compared to many of his peers in our socioeconomic class. He was far from spoiled. Rather, he was grateful for everything he had, and often said so. He loved to share, to give to others. What he cared about the most was family and friends. Erik was never a petty person with false pride. He had a big heart and soul and was quick to apologize sincerely when he said or did something hurtful, even to his siblings.

But Erik had his struggles. He suffered from learning difficulties, which made school an unwelcome and often overwhelming undertaking. Despite our encouragement and understanding, his academic shortfalls ravaged his self-esteem. Peers—and even some thoughtless teachers—called him "stupid" to his face. To make matters worse, he also suffered from Tourette's syndrome, and his odd tics and mannerisms left him vulnerable to unkind remarks. It was during his middle school years that I began to see this happy, charming, affectionate child transform into a stranger. He slowly built a shell of toughness to protect himself from a cruel world. He smiled less often and was involved in a number of fistfights at school.

And so began the darkness. It crept into his life like a toxic infection, sucking the light from his heart and soul. But this darkness was still no match for the love within.

Let me tell you all a story that highlights this perfectly. His sister, Michelle, only recently shared it with us. She and Erik were so close, they may as well have been twins. Michelle had a few tragic romances as a teen. When she was eighteen, she met Chris, the "love of her life," and vowed to marry him only a week or two after they met. This was not a happy announcement for my husband and me, because Chris . . . well, you know those guys who, at the age of thirty, are still living in their parents' basement, playing Xbox and smoking pot all night while skateboarding and drinking beer all day? If only he'd had such aspirations. Now, he's behind bars. I guess eighteen-year-old girls don't have the best judgment sometimes.

When Michelle and Chris broke off their engagement, she shared her story with Erik as they were riding in her car together. She began to sob, because to her the breakup marked the end of life as she knew it. (My husband and I also shed tears over the experience, but ours were tears of relief and joy.) No sooner had Michelle begun to cry than Erik joined in. He held her hand and sobbed with her the entire way home. It was as if he had been the victim of the breakup. When someone's heart broke, Erik's broke as well. If someone he cared about felt pain, so did he. What courage it takes to feel the pain of others. It's hard enough to bear the weight of one's own troubles without taking on the grief of others. What a heavy burden for a young, loving, sensitive boy.

By the time he was fifteen, Erik was diagnosed with bipolar disorder and was started on medication. Despite weekly sessions with both a therapist and a psychiatrist, Erik slid into a deep depression. I believe that he found solace in drugs and alcohol partly to give credence to that tough exterior, and partly to ease the pain. As parents, we did everything we could to help him feel better about himself. As with all five children, not a day went by that we didn't tell him how much we loved him and how grateful we were to have him in our lives. Eventually, Erik seemed to improve somewhat. He stopped consuming drugs and alcohol, and embarked on a career path to becoming a welder. However, as happiness seemed to elude him still, he developed an insatiable appetite for material possessions to fill the empty void: a stereo system for his truck, a new welder, equipment for a new sport or hobby, or a new bike. When he ran out of money, he pawned nearly all of his other possessions for the next "fix." He also had an intense yearning for friendship.

Sadly, Erik was well aware of the fact that many of his "friends" answered his calls only to hang up immediately once they realized it was him calling. Many regarded him as odd and quirky, and as a result, he often felt deeply lonely. I find this so ironic because Erik was so caring toward others, whether they were friends, acquaintances, or strangers. He wouldn't hesitate to give anyone the shirt off his back, and he often brought home troubled friends his age who were in need of a home-cooked meal and a place to sleep. In his twenty years here on Earth, I never heard him utter a critical or disparaging word about another person. Perhaps because of his struggles, he was one of the most compassionate, nonjudgmental people I have ever known.

Erik was misunderstood by so many. He sometimes came across as intense and disheveled. He was tormented by tics and an addiction to cigarettes. However, beneath all that exterior was a diamond in the rough. Few were kinder. Few were more loving. Few were as understanding. Few were as willing to sacrifice for others. Sometimes I felt like the only one in the world who saw Erik's real soul. This was a lonely feeling. That began to change when I received the following loving email from one of his friends after his death:

Dear Dr. Medhus,

It is with much respect and condolences that I accepted your invitation to be on your friend list [for Facebook]. I have thought about your son Erik and your family often, praying that you find any comfort possible in your egregious loss at his untimely death.

My last memory of Erik was at Starbucks. I have been employed there for three years, and this is how I came to befriend Erik.

He truly was one of my favorite Memorial (High School) students, which actually says a lot. I did not have patience (sometimes still don't) for many of their adolescent behaviors and attitudes. Erik was different than most of the students, and I was always happy to see him. He was always ready to offer a smile, or help to keep the peace on the porch when I had to ask them to behave. We chatted often at the bar or on the patio.

It was very close to his death when he came into the store seeming withdrawn, not like his usual self (at least with me).

I gave him a drink on the house, and we chatted some. I was a little concerned, but I'm embarrassed to say that I chalked it up to a bad day or a bad week. I thought, "He'll get over it." He asked me if I would be his friend on Facebook, and I was happy to say yes. He added me that day. It was only a few short days later that I got the news of his suicide. I wish that I would have listened to my instinct and tried to reach out to Erik more. He was a great kid.

I started reading your blog, and it is inspiring and heartwarming to believe that he is still with us in this earthly realm, watching over his friends and family. Though he has peace on the other side, I want you to know I still pray for your family often!

I wish I could offer much more to you; it is unfortunately the best I can give right now. Please let Erik know that I think of him fondly, and miss him too, when you have your next visit with him. May you feel his presence often, and may your memories of him be a balm to your breaking heart.

Respectfully,
Amber

When I read this letter, I couldn't help but cry. My tears were those of gratitude and joy, but also of sorrow that Erik never realized just how worthy of love he was. All of this doesn't begin to scratch the surface of who Erik was—and is. He had his imperfections, like we all do, but they paled in comparison to his many wonderful qualities.

2

ERIK'S DEATH

Then came that horrible Tuesday, the events of which created a deep chasm that divided my life into two parts: the wonderful "before" and the intolerable "after." Erik seemed to be stable and happy that day. Over the course of those last few months, he had finally found friends he could trust—friends who loved him as he loved them. My sister Teri was visiting from her home in California, and she, two of my daughters, and I planned to go out somewhere for lunch. I asked Erik if he'd like to join us, but he declined, saying he preferred to stay home and "chill." He asked how long we'd be gone, and I told him we'd return in no more than an hour.

Five minutes into the drive, I received the worst phone call of my life. Maria, our housekeeper, who had helped take care of Erik since he was sixteen months old, called to say that she had heard a "loud noise" and was scared. Although I had no reason to suspect anything, I instinctively knew. I asked her if it had sounded like a gun and she replied, "Yes." I begged her to go upstairs to check on Erik, and she did. The scream I heard moments later would forever be etched in my mind— a scream that marked the beginning of a nightmare from which we would only awaken from after months and months of tears; a scream that dashed our hopes along with our sense of inviolability. It marked the beginning of our emotional collapse into a carful of hysterics.

We were home in a matter of minutes—minutes that seemed more like decades. I was afraid to go upstairs and confront what I knew to be the tragic truth, but as a physician, I needed to be sure he was truly dead. What if he still had a pulse? Maybe I could administer CPR and save him. But upon seeing my son, sitting in his desk chair, eyes open and lifeless, with an obvious gunshot wound to the head, it was clear he was gone forever and could not be brought back to life. Only days later would I discover that he had pawned possessions and asked a twenty-one-year-old friend to purchase a handgun for him. In great despair, I flung myself into his lap, screaming like a wounded mother wolf mourning the loss of her cub. It felt like I was out of my body, peering down upon this broken shell of a woman whose hands were bathed in the blood of her own child.

The days that followed were torture. No mother should have to bury her child, much less hire a crime scene cleanup crew to pull out his carpet and scour the walls. It's amazing how one ill-fated decision to pull back that trigger a few agonizing millimeters was all it took to detonate an atom bomb in our family. Our entire family was cata-pulted into a new world of grief, bewilderment, anger, and guilt. As a mother, the effect seemed to take an even greater toll, as if the physical connection that had begun between us twenty years and nine months earlier had been ripped apart so violently that a heavy pain permeated every part of my body and soul. It leached into every cell, distorted every memory, and haunted every thought.

For months, I found it difficult to trudge outside to get the mail and newspaper. More days than not, I longed for death so that I might hold Erik in my arms once more. Grief enveloped me so deeply that I forgot I wasn't alone. My husband, my four other children, countless relatives, and close friends were also in pain. I had to make a conscious effort to encourage them to share their burden as well, to cry on my shoulder, and to lean on what little strength I had left. After months of stumbling blindly through this new and cruel darkness, I decided that enough was enough.

Although my son was dead, I was still his mother. I wanted that relationship to not only survive but to also thrive. This meant treading on dangerous territory, where answers are elusive and indistinct, and disappointment might lurk in every shadow. Somehow, I had to find the courage within to ask the tough questions: Why did he take his life when he had so much to live for? What was death like for him? Where is he now? *What* is he now? Is there an afterlife, and if so, what is it like? I resolved to find the answers.

3

ERIK'S VISITS: DREAMS, MESSAGES, AND PRANKS

After Erik's death, my entire family and I plunged into a state of numbness. We were shaken by a grief so profound that each minute seemed like an eternity. Making the funeral arrangements—from choosing a casket and burial plot to deciding what clothes he should wear in his perpetual sleep—was agony. Every decision was gut wrenching and seemingly insurmountable. All I wanted to do was lie down in a corner and sob. I was so grateful for Rune's inner strength. He, too, was in pain, but society mandates that the man must keep a stiff upper lip and muddle through on his own somehow. Men tend to be the silent, neglected grievers—the broken warriors who need just as much support and comfort as women.

In all the tragedy and turmoil, however, Erik came to provide us with comfort three times, thus initiating our journey in communicating with him in the afterlife. The second night after his death, he came to my husband in an uncharacteristically vivid dream. In that dream, they were both standing near Rune's new Ford F-350, a truck that my son had drooled over with great pride. Then Erik said in joyous excitement, "I feel so wonderful! I'm so light and free. It's an amazing feeling. Here, Pappa, feel." When Erik reached out to grab his father's hands, Rune was overcome with a sense of intense euphoria, unlike any sensation he'd had before.

It was a feeling of joy, love, comfort, lightness, and freedom that simply cannot be described in our limited human language. After a few moments, Erik let go of Rune's hands, leaned toward him, and said, "This is what I felt like before." Rune then felt the deep despair and darkness that had long tormented Erik. The world felt heavy and unwelcoming. Through this dream, Rune knew Erik was trying to convey that he was fine and was, in fact, happy for the first time in years. In that moment, our family's healing process began.

The second time Erik made himself known after his passing was to his grandfather, José. Let me preface this by saying that my father has never truly believed in life after death. To him, when the body dies, so does the soul; we all simply turn to dust. There is no immortality. There is no God. There is no Heaven. Yet, three days after my son's death, my father called me to say that Erik had come to him. I could tell by his voice that he was quite shaken. He said that, while he was wide awake, Erik appeared to him. Then, he transformed into a four-or five-year-old version of himself, crawled into his grandfather's lap and snuggled against his chest.

My father felt, without a doubt, that Erik's presence was real. He felt the warmth of his grandson's small body and the love that emanated from his presence. After a few moments, Erik looked up at his grandfather and recited a Spanish proverb that essentially translates as "things come in threes." Erik's visit challenged the very foundation of the staunch beliefs my father had held for decades. As for the meaning behind the proverb, I wondered to myself if Erik was preparing my father and my mother—both in their eighties—for their own transition into the afterlife. Or perhaps he was foretelling the three visits he would make in so many days.

The third visit occurred a few weeks after Erik died. My eldest daughter, Kristina, shared this interesting experience with me—an incident that provided evidence of Erik's burgeoning skills with energy manipulation. She was up late studying one night, as medical students are notoriously known to do. As part of a new ritual, she lit a candle in honor of Erik and placed it on her desk by her study materials. Without warning, the candle's flame began to dance erratically. Now, this might not seem so weird to you, but since it was a chilly night, the air-conditioning was off. There was no breeze, no source for air currents. Kristina even covered her mouth with a sheet of paper and turned her head to the side to make sure her breath was not causing the air to stir and therefore the flame to jump. At that same moment, she also felt Erik's presence strongly and knew he was up to his old mischief as a prankster, playing a practical joke.

To test her little brother's new abilities, Kristina asked Erik to still the flame. It froze in place instantly. After waiting for a few seconds, she asked him to make the flame leap upward. It did. In fact, the flame seemed to obey every order she barked out, without fail: "Stop . . . Move . . . Grow . . . Shrink." Finally, Kristina asked Erik to move the flame slowly to one side. She was floored when it gradually shifted sideways until the base of the flame disconnected completely from the wick, seeming to float in midair. Kristina felt a sense of awe and comfort knowing that Erik is still around and, better yet, has retained his well-known reputation as an accomplished jokester.

As the weeks passed, many people, including family and friends, reported visits from Erik, most of them vivid, tangible, and accompanied by a complete certainty that his presence is real. My younger sister, Laura, always had a special connection with Erik, perhaps because they shared some of the same struggles, or perhaps because they shared the same philosophy of life. Whatever the reasons, she was particularly devastated by his death. I'm certain Erik sensed her grief and came to comfort her in the wee hours one morning. Here's Laura's poignant story of her visit with her nephew:

Erik's presence was sitting on the porch with me, and I felt very calm and sure of his being there with me. I told him how much he was missed, and felt like he understood the grief we all were experiencing because of his passing. There was so much empathy and compassion radiating from him. He was certainly "all knowing." I asked Erik to watch over his mom, dad, brother, sisters, and the rest of the family, and to let them know that he was happy. I told him that I understood his pain and suffering in life, and I could tell that he had finally found peace. We sat in silence for about thirty or forty minutes. I reached over the patio table and held his hand and squeezed it. Then I told him that I knew he was going to be busy visiting his family, but he could come visit Jim and me anytime. I told him I loved him and was grateful for his visit. Then he left. I felt better afterward.

All of these visits were of great comfort to my family, although I did wonder selfishly why he had not appeared to me, his own mother. It seemed I was the only member of the family who had not actually seen Erik. Why? No grief could possibly be as profound and heart wrenching as that of a mother who has lost a child, and I grew to suspect that there was a heavy cloak draping my mind as well as my heart, blocking all of Erik's attempts to communicate with me. I decided that I would just have to be patient. A month later, my prayers were answered in the form of a dream. Erik appeared before me in my kitchen with a sweet, loving smile on his face. I folded him into my arms and held him for a long time. This was different from any other dream I had ever experienced. I could smell his skin. I could feel my lips grazing the stubble on his cheek. I could feel him against my chest. It was unquestionably real—nothing like the vague sensations in a typical dream.

Many assume that the spirits of our departed loved ones enjoy staying in contact with us, trying to get our attention in numerous ways in an effort to continue their relationship with us. The easiest ways for them to do so are by visiting us in dreams and by manipulating electrical energy. Some will appear on computer screens, some will make the lights flicker, some will cause a radio to play a meaningful song, some will call us on the telephone, and some will cause our appliances to go haywire. In my readings on spiritual matters concerning life after death, I have found that there is a general consensus as to how newly untethered souls can communicate with loved ones here on Earth. As I mentioned earlier, contact in dreams is one way, and another is the manipulation of energy. As they learn how to control their energy, souls communicate with us in less subtle manners—even through tangible, physical manifestations.

Physical Visits

As membership to the *Channeling Erik* blog grew, Erik's visits and pranks began to spread beyond family and friends. Now, he is a global phenomenon, with connections in the Philippines, Ireland, the United Kingdom, Russia, and other countries. It seems that the only prerequisite for experiencing some of Erik's mischief is a willingness to visit the *Channeling Erik* blog and begin to read. It also seems that the more individuals interact through comments and forum threads on the blog, the greater the chance of being visited—or getting "punked," as Erik would probably put it. As Erik's reach grows, so does his repertoire. Erik has a whole gamut of tricks up his sleeves.

Erik's most spectacular visits are those in which he appears physically to us on the earthly plane. Because there is such a huge gap between spirits' vibrational frequency and ours, souls are usually required to lower theirs, so that it is within the visible part of the electromagnetic spectrum, and for us to raise ours—to meet them halfway, so to speak. Damien, a young man from Ireland, was one of the first blog members to share his experience of being visited by Erik. A paramedic who planned to emigrate to Canada to be with his long-distance girlfriend, Damien was raised by his mother to keep his mind and his heart open to communication from the spiritual realm. Before being visited by

Erik, Damien had experienced the presence of his two deceased sisters. The following is his account of his visit with Erik:

On Sunday night last, I was lying in bed, just after reading the blog. I felt a presence and a strong American accent in my head. I asked if it was Erik. He answered, "Yeah, it is. What's up?" I then started a dialogue with him, asking him about his experience. . . . He is such a kind, genuine soul. . . . I decided at this point to confirm that it was indeed Erik. Knowing he has been practicing with energy to make his presence known, I asked him to move something. No sooner had I stopped speaking than a loud bang came from downstairs. With everyone else asleep and the cat out of the house, I knew instantly it was Erik.

As my conversation continued with him, he suddenly remarked, "That singer you know, she's a real catch." He was referring to my girlfriend in Canada, who is a successful singer. Due to long distance, the relationship is "on hold." But Erik went on to say that we are soul mates and have been together in past lives. He told me that, in my first two lives, I searched for her; in my third and fourth, we spent our lives together. In the sixth, I died in World War II, shortly after we met. This is my seventh life, he assured me. Then the most amazing thing happened, which has left me amazed, truly amazed. Erik asked me if I wanted to know how far my girl was from me right at that moment. I said sure. . . . He said, "She is 4,056 kilometers from you right now," and then he said, "Go on, check. I dare ya," with a really cheeky grin on his face. :) So I Googled the distance from my address to where she was and it was 4,050 kilometers. I laughed and told him I'd give him the six kilometers. It was incredible. I had a meeting [at] work over something the following morning and I was worried about it. Erik told me to remain calm and not to worry, that I wouldn't need the job 'cause I'd be leaving the country soon.

He then brought my sisters forward to talk, and he assured me my girl loved me and that she was waiting to hold me; and we would be ok. He assured me I'm on [the path of] my destiny and am supposed to be a healer. (Your son is incredible and a true gift to this world. You both are.)

I thanked him and felt exhausted and went to sleep. Sure enough, next morning, the meeting went well. I thanked him the following night. I asked him why he appears to a lot of people and helps them. He said simply, "You took the time to read my story. I wanna help you out." I was very taken aback. He's a true gent. He then went on to tell me I need to cherish the time with my friends and family, as I'll be leaving the country very soon. The next day in your blog, you commented on how he said he was busy helping people the night before. He truly was.

I hope you and your family are doing well. . . . I have long believed in the afterlife, reincarnation. . . . Erik and you have confirmed everything I believe in. Thank you. It certainly makes it easier to deal with death when we can't save patients. I cannot say thank you enough for being strong enough and brave enough to post this blog. I cannot wait to see what further insights Erik and you have for us in our search for enlightenment.

Yours Truly,
Damien

Visiting as Another Person

I have heard that our deceased loved ones often contact us through children and even animals. At other times, they contact through look-alikes. They want us to know that they are always with us, that this three-dimensional world we live in and perceive with our five senses is but the tip of the iceberg, and that our true existence is in a larger, more meaningful reality. In many ways, this domain can be considered our real home—a domain that, as souls, we return to with great anticipation and joy. In this next story, Erik works with a child to send a message to a woman he deeply loved.

Erik had a deep crush on a girl named Stacy, whom he met when they were both around fourteen years old. She was beautiful and kind, and saw the lovely soul that was my son, even when he was in the gangly, pimply stage. Sadly, she moved with her family to the West Coast, so Erik and Stacy had to communicate from then on through texts and online messages. Worse yet, she eventually left him for another man, had a baby, and denied him a happy future with the girl of his dreams. I say this in a very tongue-in-cheek manner, as Erik and Stacy never had that kind of relationship. Their friendship was strictly platonic, but they did adore each other immensely.

Stacy was devastated upon hearing the news of Erik's death. Shortly after he died, he came to me in a dream. In that dream, he told me that he was going to watch over Stacy and her little boy forever, and he asked me to pass this information along to her. In the morning, I found Stacy on Facebook and sent her the message as he instructed. The next day, she replied with a response that floored me.

Stacy said that she had been thinking of Erik a lot lately and asked him to help her land a job she applied for at a day-care center. Sure enough, she was hired. On her first day, she was feeling very nervous because the staff and kids were all strangers to her. However, as soon as she crossed the threshold, a little boy ran up to her, flung his arms around her legs, and said, "Hi, I'm Erik, and I love you with all of my heart!" Right then, she knew with great certainty that my son was communicating with her through a stranger. She sat down and sobbed. It was his way of saying, "I'll always love and protect you and your family."

Touching and Tickling

About three months after Erik died, he told me (through spiritual translator Kim O'Neill) that he would, at the very least, send a message to me by creating a sensation of goose bumps on a leg, an arm, or on some part of my head. I found this hard to believe because, from the medical perspective, "regional goose bumps" just don't happen. Generalized goose bumps over much of the body, yes, but on only one side or one limb? Nah. Plus, I have never been highly attuned to my body, as I'm more cerebral and internally focused. Furthermore, I just don't get goose bumps very often, even when I'm out in sub-zero weather in my husband's home country of Norway, so I wasn't sure I would recognize it if it did happen.

A few months ago, I was sitting in the waiting room while my car went through the car wash—a biannual tradition necessary to scoop the lint-covered gummy bears out of the cup holders before the mess becomes petrified beyond hope. After reading last week's newspaper scattered on the coffee table, I suddenly thought about Erik's agreement and felt his presence nearby. *This is odd*, I thought. My husband was racing his motorcycle on the track at that moment, so I figured Erik would be hanging out with him all day. Like his pappa, Erik is a big motor head. *Hmm*, I thought, *I've got to take advantage of this rarity. Let's see what this boy's got!*

So I asked Erik to make me feel goose bumps on the right side of my head. It took a couple of minutes, but just as I was about to give up all hope that it would happen, I felt it. The sensation was so strong that I thought my scalp was about to crawl off my skull—in the most pleasant of ways, mind you. *Good job, Erik!* I said. *Now, make me feel goose bumps on the other side of my head.* Minutes passed. Nothing. Zip. So, with a shrug of indifference, I gave up. I figured he had left to join his father at the track. Oh well. It was wonderful while it lasted.

Satisfied, I closed my eyes and, with a warm smile on my face, sent Erik my love. I envisioned the arms of my soul wrapping around him and drawing him to my heart. In my mind's eye, I hugged him, kissed him gently on his forehead, and said, *Erik, I couldn't be prouder of you, sweetie. You're helping so many people here on Earth. I love you so very much.* During those moments, my thoughts were focused like a laser beam on the intense love and pride I felt for my son.

A few moments later, I started to feel goose bumps on the left side of my head. This took me by surprise, because I had all but forgotten about my request. My jaw dropped in amazement. Could this be happening a second time? The scientist in me thought, *Okay, let's test this again.* The mother in me thought, I hope he doesn't think I'm making too many demands. Nothing like the whole "Dance, monkey boy, dance!" thing to make any teenage kid roll his eyes in annoyance. But in the interest of confirming my hypothesis, I took a deep breath and made my third request: *Erik, make me feel goose bumps on my right arm.* Minutes passed . . . nothing. Hmm. Okay, so maybe it was a coincidence. So what? I still enjoyed feeling the love I have for him, so I sent a second wave of tender thoughts and visions for several minutes.

Eventually, my mind started to wander down a crazy detour littered with a series of thought potholes: *Where the heck is my car? Wonder if the kids unloaded the dishwasher? What should I cook for dinner tonight?* While I was preoccupied by a long string of these menial thoughts, my right arm abruptly began to develop goose bumps. Intense ones. I was so overwhelmed with gratitude and love, tears of joy began to roll down my cheeks. Clean car, miracle from Erik: my day was complete.

To spare the waiting room full of customers from further alarm and discomfort, I quietly left to sit outside on the curb. I had to soak this all in, to savor the moment. Then, something compelled me to turn my head to the right, where, lo and behold, a beautiful dragonfly sat calmly beside me. It stayed there for a long time, just watching me with its big bug-eyed expression. Just like he has done many times since his death, Erik used something beautiful to make contact and give me yet another sign of his presence. From that day forward, Erik has often chosen to visit me and others as a gorgeous dragonfly, even during the winter months. Also, I discovered only recently that several members of the family have experienced these intense, regional goosebumps intermittently but only after Erik's death. In retrospect, I believe Erik's abilities have been strengthened by my love and the love of his other family members and friends. After all, love is energy, and powerful energy at that.

Nasty Smells

Erik still has a sense of humor like the one he had in his corporeal existence on Earth. One of Erik's signature pranks is creating noxious fumes: marijuana or cigarette smoke, stinky-sock odor, skunk spray, bong water, and oh so much more. In this account, blog member Bec shares her "stinky Erik" encounter, mixed in with a goose bumps experience so like my own. What makes this story more amazing is the fact that she was new to our blog community and had no prior knowledge of Erik's particular brand of irreverent pranks.

Hi Elisa,

My name is Rebecca (most of my friends and family call me Bec), and I have to tell you that I am so in love with what you and Erik are doing! I log on to the website every day for my "daily dose" of enlightenment and to see how you are doing. Erik is amazing and you are an inspiration, Elisa! I am in awe of your displays of courage, openness, and at times, vulnerability. It's truly moving and makes me (and others) want to be better people and treat people with the love that every living thing on this planet needs and deserves.

Well, I started at the beginning of your blog and read every word up to your first . . . session (I was at work, so I was sneaking to read it and didn't get very far). I work two jobs (an oral surgeon's office during the day and I tend bar at night), and oftentimes, I stay at my mom's house on the days that I work both places (I work for cash, and coming in late by myself scares me a little). If my mom can, she waits up for me. We usually have a glass of wine and talk about anything and everything. It was early Saturday morning (about 3:00 AM), and my mom and I were doing our usual "garage" meeting when I began telling her about your blog.

I told her about you, Erik, and Kim. She was fascinated! Well, as I was talking about Erik, I began to get goose bumps all over my body. They were rather intense goose bumps—even the tiny hairs on my face were standing up. I showed my mom, and she remarked that it was ninety-one degrees; why would I have chills? It was a little weird. We continued to talk about Erik (I still had the goose bumps), and then out of the blue my mom said, "Ew! Ugh! Someone must have hit a skunk. That's awful. Do you smell that?" Of course I did. I joked and said maybe one of the neighbors was smoking weed. As fast as it came, it left, and so did my goose bumps. We continued to talk about you, Erik, and Kim for a little while longer.

Oh boy, was I amazed the next day at work when I logged on to your site and picked up reading where I left off. A few posts into your blog, I read that Erik said he was going to identify himself by the pungent smell of bong water (which I find hilarious, because I totally have that kind of sense of humor with my mom), and then I read even further. I got to the part about the goose bumps and had to pick my mouth up off the floor. I called my mom to share that with her, and I knew I had to write you. Can you ask Erik if that was him? Was he trying to bring someone through to us? [Indeed, in a subsequent session with Jamie, he confirmed that it was him.]

Also, this past Saturday, I was cleaning house and stepped outside to take a break, when out of the blue, a dragonfly started fluttering around me. It hung around me for about five minutes, and then fluttered off. I remember your post about that too; it instantly made me think of you and Erik.

Please keep doing what you're doing, and I would love to hear back from you. I'm sorry if this is poorly written. I'm sneaking this at work.

Thank you for your time, Elisa. I am thanking Erik too!

XOXOXO, Bec

Moving Objects

According to Erik, there's not much an untethered soul can't do. He explains that spirits can move objects by altering the energy field in front of or behind them, so it didn't surprise me when he began to test this skill—one of my personal favorites when it comes to Erik's pranks. Incidentally, Erik often pranks women on whom he has crushes in this way. Blog member Randi shares her Erik story, proving that Erik still loves the ladies and is augmenting his ability to manipulate and expand energy to impress them.

What's particularly funny about this prank is that Randi confesses to have obsessive compulsive disorder, so clearly, Erik was testing her tolerance and patience!

I want to share some weird stuff that happened yesterday—I can't help but wonder whether it's Erik pranking me. I know that last summer he visited me in the form of a foul smell, but this was a little different. I spent the day putzing around my apartment (our office was closed), cleaning and doing some work on my computer.

Anyway, as I went into my kitchen, I noticed that one of the drawers was open. I was a little puzzled, because I never leave them open, but I closed it and didn't think much of it. A few minutes later, I noticed that it was open again. So, I shut it. Then, a couple of hours later, the same thing happened with one of the bathroom drawers. I actually wondered if maybe I slammed them and the force popped them back out, so I tested it—but even closing them at different forces kept them closed. And I'm not the type to leave cabinets and drawers open—especially so much in one day.

Then, later, when I got home from my run, I threw my headphones on the middle of the counter. About thirty minutes later, I noticed that they were hanging on the counter by the earbuds, with the wire dangling down toward the floor. It would have been near impossible for that to have just happened, considering where I left them on the counter.

If it wasn't Erik goofing off in my apartment and trying to confuse me, it was definitely someone else. This stuff was just too weird. But, by the end, I was laughing about it.

This all came the day after I was sitting on my couch, watching television, and my eyes were drawn to a big armchair I have in the living room. I suddenly got a sensation that the armchair was important, like someone was sitting there, or someone should have been or would be sitting there. Who knows, maybe Erik decided to hang out with me for a couple of days and was keeping me and my dog company during the Golden Globes!

During our first summer without Erik, and after twenty years of seeing our kitchen abused by our five children and a variety of pets, we decided to bear the expense and remodel. Although we were able to keep most of our appliances, we had to replace our downdraft vent because it was no longer functional. On its side were irresistible buttons that made it go up and down and up and down, and the kids, particularly Erik, just couldn't keep their fingers to themselves. Another important part of this story is that Erik adored our kitchen. First, he loved to cook. Second, when he had nothing else better to do, he would pace around the kitchen's center island, his arms crossed. He'd pace and pace and pace until I'd start to get motion sickness from watching him and had to beg him to stop. Our old tile is a testament to the wear and tear he caused. I actually miss seeing the grooved track he made.

That said, after the new vent was installed, it seemed to work perfectly. Then, when my husband walked into the kitchen from the backyard one day, the vent mysteriously began to rise. He was alone in the kitchen and was at least twenty feet away. At first, he thought nothing of it and called the technician to replace all of the parts that are responsible for the vent's movement, including the pad with all the buttons and wiring. You'd think that would have fixed the problem, but no. The next night when my husband entered the kitchen, the vent slowly began to rise again!

Electrical appliances simply don't turn off and on by themselves. Imagine if your blender suddenly started to whir? This would probably unnerve you enough to fill it full of margarita fixings with a little extra tequila for good measure. We are certain that this is Erik, trying to tell us, "Hey, sorry it's been a while, but I'm here." He's probably still pacing around the kitchen island from time to time, wearing out my brand new tile.

Ever mechanically minded, Erik soon branched out from kitchen appliances to plumbing fixtures. While one of my daughters was in my bathroom ravaging through my makeup drawer, the sink faucet suddenly turned on. By itself. Michelle was at least three or four feet away. She knew immediately that it was Erik, up to his old tricks again, and admonished him in her usual tongue-in-cheek manner. They've always been close and loved teasing and playing with one another. I suppose some things never change, even after death.

Erik also developed a penchant for throwing food around. He often accompanies spirit translator Robert Burke to the grocery store, begging for whatever cereal has the most sugar and dyes. Once, he even threw a bag of Twizzlers into Robert's shopping cart from a shelf three or four feet away.

During our 2011 vacation to Destin, Florida, Erik came through with several of his usual pranks. The best prank of all happened while we were eating breakfast at the Waffle House. Many of you might be familiar with this pint-sized restaurant, where hash slinging is a cherished art. The tables, however, are equally pint-sized, so squeezing six bodies around a table designed for four takes some doing. Eating in cramped quarters takes finesse too; and it helps to Velcro your elbows to your waists. Sometimes it works, but sometimes it doesn't. That morning, the casualties of Erik's penchant for having fun with food included: a spilled large Coke; a freshly served biscuit, smothered in sausage gravy—and drenched in water; and my son-in-law Shane's All-Star Special (bacon, eggs, toast, hash browns, and waffle) sliding right across the table and into his lap. We all laughed, knowing it was bound to be one of Erik's pranks.

A month later, Robert Burke and I went out to dinner with my friend Marjie, who had lost her eldest son, Tommy, to a drunk driving accident a year or two before Erik's death. Tommy was a "live for the moment" guy who had more friends than you could shake a stick at. We were sipping on frozen margaritas at Lupe Tortillas, sharing stories of Erik and Tommy, while Robert was busy relaying information from Erik and Tommy to the both of us, since, according to him, they hovered around our table. Then, without warning, the pepper mill tumbled off the table and onto the floor. We didn't think much of it, because the waiter was nearby. Maybe his white apron had brushed against it. Robert picked it up and set it on the table, this time far from the edge. Moments later, the pepper mill flew off the table again. Robert began to laugh. I'm sure the sight of Marjie and me, with our mouths agape and eyes the size of saucers, fueled his laughter. He said Tommy and Erik each had a finger on the pepper mill and were pushing it toward the table's edge together. Ghostly teamwork from a pair of consummate pranksters.

After a few gasps and giggles, we admonished the boys in jest and continued our conversation. Our dinner came along with another round of margaritas. *Whoosh,* off flew the plastic stand that holds the leaflet of the day's specials. We all saw it slide off the table and onto the floor. It was at least four to five inches from the edge, so we couldn't blame gravity alone. It wasn't the margaritas either, because we had barely started to sip our second round. Nope, Robert confirmed it was the Spirit Finger Duo at work.

Hiding Objects

Erik loves hiding objects from family, friends, and even blog members, much to everyone's annoyance. He says that all it takes is working with the energy around that object to conceal it. Think "invisibility cloak," Harry Potter–style.

Erik also loves leveraging his pranks against our flaws. For instance, I have this thing about being organized. *Very* organized. I have lists for everything—even lists of my lists. This personality trait probably evolved because of my ADHD, as a means of finding order in my own personal inner chaos. I don't know whether I could have survived medical school otherwise. Throw in five kids (six, if you count my husband), and my obsessive compulsion for organization ramps up into high gear. I keep my daily schedule on my iPhone, but I duplicate the day's activities on an index card, which, like a newly hatched chick, never strays far from my side.

Naturally, kids love to pick on a parent's flaw for their own entertainment, and I've certainly given them lots of material for that. Erik, in particular, used to laugh at my index cards, especially when they had things on them like "open mail," "bathe kids," and "make tomorrow's index card." He always pulled my leg with comments like, "What? You forgot to write down 'breathe' and 'chew food'!"

On the day of the prank in question, I took the kids to school as I usually do, and when I returned home, I noticed the index card, which I usually keep in my purse, was missing. I went back out to my car to check the console, but it wasn't there. So I looked throughout the house: the kids' bedrooms, the bathrooms, under the sofas, in the trashcans. Nothing. *Hmm. That's weird*, I thought to myself, feeling mildly irritated. Determined to prevail, I went back out to my car, checked under and between the seats, in the side-door pockets, on the ground around and under the car, and so on. Nothing. The garage? Nothing.

The dog-food canister? Nothing. All the trashcans again? Nothing. All of the rooms in the house? Nothing. I even emptied out the contents of my purse, which basically included my wallet, sunglasses, lipstick, cell phone, and comb. Nothing.

Panic started to creep in. I could make another card, but what if I had written down something critical that had not been entered into my iPhone? I looked one more time—everywhere—and came up with a big fat zero once again. At that point, I had to reluctantly resign myself to the possibility that my precious index card had vanished into thin air. Begrudgingly, I made another one, straining doggedly not to forget a single reminder. I did so hurriedly, because I had planned to visit with my parents across town and needed to get there long before my father left for the gym for his daily workout. But as I started to grab my purse, I saw a flash of white sticking out about two inches. My heart stopped. In my mind's eye, I saw Erik's face, with that classic mischievous smile of his—the smile that says, "You're punked!" I reached inside and pulled out the target of my half-hour-long search: the infamous index card. I knew he had pulled a meaningful prank to let me know that he is, indeed, present and as sneaky as ever. Mind you, I had searched my purse three times, once emptying out its sparse contents. There is no way I could have missed a white, four-by-six index card in a small black purse! Furthermore, I was the only person in the house, and my cats, lacking opposable thumbs, could not possibly take the rap.

Playing with Electricity

Erik also enjoys manipulating electricity for many of his pranks. Here's an email I received from Robert Burke while I was visiting relatives in Norway:

> *I was speaking to [your sister] Laura today, and while we were talking, Erik popped in and flushed the toilet. He got a kick outta*

doing that, mostly because I got a confused look on my face and then grinned when I heard him laughing and slapping his knee. I didn't mention it to Laura, because at the time we were deep in a discussion and I didn't wanna lose focus. Erik says that was precisely why he did it. He LOVES trying to throw me off my game! Oh, and Erik wants to know if the floors were warm enough for y'all there in the cabin. I assume he must have been up to something or he wouldn't have brought it up . . . heehee . . .

Big hugs and lots of love to everyone!

Robert

Although Erik enjoys tampering with plumbing, as you can see, the reason this email is so amazing is that, several days before, the warming cables in the floor of the main bathroom went totally haywire for the first time ever. Despite being at the proper setting, they heated up so much that the ambient temperature in the room was eighty-nine degrees, and it felt like we were walking on hot coals. Rune had to reset the entire system. Our first thought was, "Erik, you little sneak!" This event was one of Erik's classic calling cards. No one but us, five thousand miles away, could have known about this electrical malfunction. It was not posted anywhere. Furthermore, not many would know that the floors in this remote little mountain cabin could (and should) heat up.

Although this was by far my favorite of Erik's tricks using electricity, he also pranks people by creating havoc with their cell phones, house alarms, electric car locks, and radio recording equipment, to mention a few.

Telephone Calls

The deceased do communicate with us by telephone on occasion, but this phenomenon is not very common. A few months ago, I was practicing my communications with Erik. First, I told my brain to "shut down," a command it obeys only with great reluctance. Then I proceeded with my usual greetings of love, gratitude, and longing.

No sooner had I posed my first few questions than the phone rang, interrupting my focus. I felt really irritated by the intrusion, because it seems to happen like clockwork; the phone will be completely silent until I begin. Furthermore, I felt even more frustrated when I saw "unavailable" on the caller ID. Fuming, I waited for whatever message the telemarketer was going to leave on my answering machine. But what I heard made my heart stop. Although there was some static, it was clearly Erik's voice: "Hey, it's Erik. It's me, Erik." Then the line disconnected. I raced over to the machine to replay the recording, but the message count read zero.

Frantically, I pushed the "play messages" button anyway and heard, "You have no new messages." Why hadn't it recorded what I'd clearly heard? That machine records everything, even the dial tone when the caller fails to hang up within a millisecond following my greeting. So, I dialed the number on the caller ID, which was thirteen digits long, and received the message, "The number you have dialed is out of service."

Manifesting Objects from Thin Air

Oftentimes, our deceased loved ones manifest objects in the afterlife, and then manipulate the energy of that object so that the vibrational frequency is low enough to appear in our three-dimensional world. Sometimes they drop coins; sometimes they drop white feathers; other times, they drop items that are meaningful to the recipient.

Recently, my daughter Michelle and I went on errands together. Both the driver's and passenger's doors of her car have places to hold a drink and other things, as is the case in most cars. Since we were going to the bank first, I put my two checks to be deposited, my precious index card with a (long) list of to-dos, and a pen in that side compartment. After making my deposits, I put my receipts in the compartment too, so I would remember to log them in my check register. Then we drove to Russo's Pizza to have a lovely outdoor lunch. We intended to go directly from lunch to the grocery store, but nature called for my granddaughter, Arleen. You don't mess around with this when a toddler is in the midst of potty training, so we took her to the restroom in the restaurant. But no, she insisted on going in her pink potty at my house, so we drove back home.

When we parked the car in my garage, I took everything out of the side compartment: pen, index card, and receipts. Then, true to my compulsive nature, I swept my fingers up and down the compartment to make sure I had everything. I knew I did, so I don't know what the heck I was expecting to find—a gold nugget, perhaps? Whatever. I went inside, put Arley on the potty, and recorded my deposits in the check register.

When we got back into the car, I glanced at the supposedly empty side compartment and saw a shiny dime glaring back at me. Where did that come from? There was absolutely no dime there ten minutes earlier. My OCD fingertips can attest to that. I asked Michelle if she had, for some crazy reason, decided to go around to the passenger side and slip some sort of donation on my side, but no, of course she hadn't. She had a special coin carrier in her drink holder, to keep her spare change. She saw the dime, shrugged her shoulders, and said, "I'm getting that it's from Erik." Then, I plucked the dime between my thumb and index finger, and *poof*—it disappeared completely. Vanished. Dematerialized between my fingers.

This both startled and delighted Michelle and me, and when we both searched the compartment with our fingers and our eyes, we came up with nothing. Not only that, there was no crease, no fold, no hiding place into which the dime could have slunk. In her mind's eye, Michelle saw Erik laughing hard, slapping his knee, and commenting on how hilarious we both looked as we frantically combed the small compartment for a measly ten cents, as though it were the Hope Diamond.

When I told my father about this wonderful miracle, he laughed and said that Erik should try to materialize money *without* taking it away. Forget the pennies (and dimes) from Heaven; a few C-notes might come in handy. Don't you spirits know that we have inflation over here?

As you can imagine, these dreams, pranks, and visits rocked the very core of my belief system. As a scientist and a doctor, I had always felt that, for something to be real, it must be measurable by one or more of our five senses. It had to be touched or tasted or smelled or seen or heard, or at the very least, demonstrate a definitive effect on another object. Everything else was unknowable and therefore belonged to the category of mysticism. But after all of this tangible evidence of the soul's survival after death, I see things differently. My paradigm shifted radically, inspiring me to dig much deeper for clues, answers, facts— anything that would restore the clarity I had lost.

In the months that followed, I voraciously read everything I could get my hands on about the subject, including books written by physicists and other scientists, as well as books written by spirit communicators and translators. I must have read a hundred books, which weigh heavily on my now-sagging bookshelves. But not only was I determined to redefine my concept of reality, I was also determined to find out just where my son was. If only I knew that all-important "where," I had some hope of communicating with him so that we could continue the wonderful relationship we enjoyed while he was alive.

4

OUR NEW RELATIONSHIP ACROSS THE VEIL

It is natural to grasp for contact of any sort with a lost loved one. Years before, however, I would have considered communicating through a spirit translator to be a little wacky—great fodder for jokes, even. But when Erik died, things I once doubted became urgent lifelines that I clung to in hope. In spite of my voracious reading, I was skeptical about the soul's survival after death, but when I spoke to Erik through Kim O'Neill, I felt it was truly him. His personality, his wit, his manner of speaking: it was *all* Erik. Furthermore, she conveyed details she could not possibly have known, such as the fact that he suffered from bipolar disorder as a teenager, or that he had killed himself while sitting in a chair at his desk in his bedroom.

One of the first assurances Erik expressed when we truly spoke for the first time after his death was that we, his parents, had done everything we could to prevent it. He said he had contemplated suicide for many years and just wanted to make certain he did it in a way that would ensure his passing. In the months before, he had even researched all sorts of suicide methods on the internet. Although he thought about taking an overdose of pills, one of his biggest fears was that he would survive but remain impaired for the rest of his life. In the end, Erik felt that shooting himself in the head assured him the biggest guarantee of "success." Next, he had to find a moment when he felt sure we would not be in the house when the gun went off, which, as we know, he did succeed at doing.

I'm not sure why I felt so compelled to reconstruct every minute detail of that terrible day and why I wanted to know *everything*—and I mean everything—that was going through Erik's mind before he died. Maybe this is normal; I have no idea. I was treading on new ground, so I'm not sure whether these were typical mental ruminations for a bereaved parent. It's almost as if I wanted to "think it to death" so that it would lose some of its overwhelming emotional charge. In that first session with Kim, Erik discussed why he chose to take his life the way he did and what his last thoughts were before he pulled the trigger. He said he wasn't afraid to die; it was living that terrified him. He went on to describe his first moments after death: the painlessness, the euphoria, and the freedom, followed by the horror of what he had done and the profound grief that was sure to follow in its wake. And, to his dismay, he witnessed it all.

In my ongoing struggle with my deep-seated skepticism, I have often questioned the validity of the information from any spirit translator, even though those I have worked with have recounted things that only I could know. That said, I decided to hold sessions with several world-renowned spirit translators in search of ironclad proof. Little did I know then that faith is an internal tug-of-war, not an external fight. Months after Erik's first description of his own death, I did what any rational, skeptical person would do: I sought a second opinion.

That second opinion manifested in the form of spirit translator Jamie Butler. The skeptic in me sought confirmation and consistency of information. The mother in me wanted some assurance that my child had not suffered during his transition. So I intended for my questions to be pointed and probing. In this transcript of the conversation between Jamie, Erik, and myself, Erik provides considerable detail about the circumstances and experience of his death, perhaps because he's had more time to orient himself and to reflect on the event, or perhaps because I had found a truly gifted translator who was as accurate and receptive as they come. Never before had I met a translator so free of filters. And Jamie and Erik seemed to enjoy such a playful and loving relationship that I found myself grinning widely through this session, and through the many sessions that came after. For these reasons, all of my subsequent sessions with Jamie provided the soothing balm I needed for the battle scars that seemed to be my constant companion.

Erik Describes His Own Death

Me: Erik, can you describe death and what happens right afterward, in great detail—at least what happens for most? I know everybody's death is different, but just give me whatever generalities you can.

[Long pause as Jamie listens to him]

Jamie: Okay. Hmm. I think he's smoked out or something!

Me: Uh-oh!

[Jamie and I giggle.]

Jamie: He's laughing.

Me: He's going to go out for some ethereal nachos later.

Jamie: Seriously! He won't include me. He won't tell me why he's giggling, so I don't know where it's coming from.

Erik: To explain death in general, I think, does it an injustice, Mom. So, remind all of the readers that death is hand-tailored to the person's living belief system. Whatever you actively believe in—nothing, God, that you face your demons before you have joy, that you become a ghost—it's going to be laid out for you.

Me: Okay, then let's talk about your death. You're dead, so let's talk about that. What were your beliefs? I never really—

Erik: God, aren't *you* rude!

Me: I'm sorry, but let's talk about—

Erik: Put this down before we change subjects, because people are gonna ask "Why is it based on your individual belief systems?" And you need to let them know that they're the tool. The physical body is the luggage. It contains the spirit. When the body dies, it becomes a soul. It leaves the body, and that soul is then kind of contained in consciousness. That character that you built, all those intangibles, what made you laugh—

Jamie (to Erik): Yes, your personality. Got it.

Erik: And so to move through these dimensions to get to Home, Heaven, whatever the hell you wanna call it, it's gotta do that through that conscious element that you set up—that belief system that you set up. That's gonna be told to be there. That's the basis. Now, you're asking me what I believed in. I don't really fucking know. It definitely wasn't all this! I learned way more about the structure of the afterlife by being here.

Me: Well, when you pulled that trigger, did you think there was going to be nothingness, or did you—

Erik: I was kind of hoping for it. I mean, really, I was so desperate to get out of my skin. I was just hoping that I could . . . (pause) [it was] kind of what I imagine [it would be like to be] a person with a puppy or a baby, [someone] who has a lack of sleep. I just wanted a good night's sleep. I just wanted some good, solid peace.

Me: Yeah. So, you were sort of hoping there was something, or you were not even thinking about it?

Erik: Wasn't even thinking about it.

Me: Did you ever think about, in your life, whether there could be something afterward?

Erik: Yeah! 'Cause you hear those ghost stories. For me, it wasn't about God or miracles. What I connected more to, which I thought was way more fucking believable, were the ghosts.

Jamie (to Erik): Really? That's kind of a neat way to think about it, right?

Me: Yeah.

Erik: 'Cause it's not like God's coming down—

Jamie (laughing): The way he says it!

Erik: It's not like God's coming to your house and fucking with your shit and knocking stuff over! No, that's the dead dude. So, you know there might be life after the one you're living in, but shit, it doesn't have to be based on a religious belief system. I had an inkling that there'd be an afterlife, but I had no fucking idea what it would contain.

Me: Okay. When you pulled that trigger, what happened right after? First of all, did it hurt?

Erik: No, I don't remember any pain. I remember the sound, but I don't remember anything touching me. Just the sound. So, I think [I told you] how you get pulled from your body?

Me: So, you felt a pulling sensation?

Erik: No, it was weird. It was like the lights went out. I had my eyes closed. I remember pulling the trigger. I remember I was quick about it. I didn't hesitate. I knew I was going to do this. This was the time. That was it. I didn't have any doubt about what I was doing. I wasn't conflicted. It's kind of like that set of mind?

Jamie (to Erik): What do you mean, "set of mind"?

Me: Mindset?

Jamie: Yeah, that.

Erik: That mindset you get when you're running a really long race, and you see the finish line.

Me: Ah, yeah.

Erik: You don't really tap into how exhausted you are or what emotions you feel. You just have your eye on the goal, and you're gonna get there. For me, I had my eye on the goal. I had to get out. I remember the feel of the gun, pulling the trigger, hearing the sound. There was darkness, and then I was looking at my body.

Me: Hmm. That must have been freaky.

Erik: Yeah. I had no clue. I did not know that I would be able to see myself. That never even crossed my mind. I really just kind of thought I would go into nothing. I wanted it to crumble. I wanted it to go away. I wanted to snuff it out.

Me: What were your emotions like when you saw your body? What did you feel?

[Pause]

Jamie (to Erik): Oh, that's the face? (To me) He just kind of went blank on me, and his mouth hung slightly open. He said that's what he felt.

Me: His jaw dropped? That sort of thing? Like, "What the fuck"?

Erik: No, no, Mom! It was wild. I didn't know what the fuck. It was more of an, "Oh. Oh." I didn't want to stay there. I didn't want to see everything, but I couldn't leave. It was like watching a bad car wreck.

Me: Oh, yeah.

Erik: But I wasn't tethered to it at all. It was bizarre.

Me: Tethered emotionally?

Erik: Yeah.

Me: What else did you feel?

Erik: I guess it was shock more than anything.

Me: Did you feel euphoria along with it?

Erik: Quiet. It was quiet. I had no pain. I didn't have any worries, and that was unsettling, because I hadn't felt that in a long time, like everything was in its right place.

Me: Oh!

Erik: So, I think it was way more unsettling than celebratory.

Me: Did you think it was cool to just fly around? Did you feel that unconditional love that a lot of people talk about?

Erik: No.

Me: Or was that when you crossed over?

Erik: Yes. When I crossed over.

Me: All right. Let's talk more then. So, you were looking at [your body], and you were like, "Wow," and there was a little bit of shock. Did you feel a little bit of, "Oh, shit? What are they going to think when they find me?"

[Long pause]

Jamie: He's really quiet. I can tell he's going through it.

[Very long pause]

Jamie: I'm telling him to take his time.

[Pause]

Erik: You know, I don't slow down to think about my death too much.

[Long pause]

Erik: To me, it was a way out. It has a lot of pain associated with it.

Me (tearing up): Uh-huh.

Erik: It's not just my pain, but my family's pain and my friends' pain.

Me: Yeah.

[Long pause. Clearly he's not comfortable.]

Me (sensing his discomfort and wanting to spare him further pain): Well, let's not dwell on it. Let's go to what happened and what it felt like when you started getting out of your room. Tell me about that.

Erik: I remember seeing my body leave.

[Pause]

Me: Your body left? Oh, when they were taking you away?

Erik: In the bag.

Me: Okay. Right.

Erik: Then I remember thinking that I needed to say good-bye.

Me: Yeah.

Erik: And if I remember right, that's when I started checking in with family members.

[Pause]

Me: That must have been painful, because we were not happy.

[Long pause]

Jamie: He's got his elbows on his knees; his hands are clasped in front of him. Very casual, but he's (pause) solemn. A little bit more solemn.

Erik: I remember finding—

[Long pause]

Jamie (with emotion): Aw. He's tearing up.

Me: Oh. We don't have to do this, baby.

Erik (teasing): Shut up, Mom.

Jamie: Tearing up, but not afraid to tell you to be quiet.

[I chuckle softly.]

Erik: When you slow down to go back through your memories, you see more. You do miss a lot when you're in the moment, like your eyes aren't big enough. I know I've told you before. I'm really sorry—for you. I'm really sorry for Pappa and for everyone else in my family.

Me (sobbing quietly): Yeah.

Erik: But I know there's one thing—I cannot apologize for my happiness.

Me: I know. I'm happy for you. I wouldn't have it any other way. If I had to choose between you being here and miserable, of course . . .

Erik: How fucked up is it, Mom, that that was my option?

Me: Yeah. I wouldn't want that to happen.

Erik: What I can't seem to figure out, when I go through it again, is why does it hurt so bad when the outcome was exactly what I was looking for?

Me (still crying): And you're happy. I mean, how could it hurt when you're happy? I'm just looking at the moment. The moment is unhappy, but the result was happy. So, we'll move past the moment. Tell me about your crossing over. I remember you said you felt like you were being tugged by your shoulders. I can't remember exactly.

Erik: Yeah. I felt like I was being pulled back. I guess I just really wasn't paying attention. It sounds like me, anyway. Like, I was looking at something I wasn't supposed to be looking at.

Me (confused): *You* were looking at something you weren't supposed to be looking at?

Jamie: He's speaking in general.

Me: Oh, okay.

Erik: That's probably why I didn't see this big gorgeous white light or, you know, hear angels sing!

Jamie (giggling): He's laughing.

[I chuckle through my tears.]

Erik: Nah, I was probably fucking doing something wrong. Probably I got jerked.

Me: Oh, I see. I see.

Erik: Yeah. *That* feeling was unspeakable. That one is like taking a body and putting it through a strainer and having all of the pieces come out on the other end, but different. Clean. I suppose it would be the feeling that [people had] back in the old times, when they thought that, if they were baptized by Jesus, everything would disappear and they'd only be good. That's really what death is.

Me: Wow. Hmm.

Erik: You really are good. You're not missing those other parts. They're still with you, but they don't play a big part of the song. You don't lose any of yourself, but what comes forward is this overwhelming sense of perfection, of being in the right place, being loved, and being able to *feel* it. Like, there's not even the tiniest doubt about what's coming your way, or whether there is some string attached, or they're just trying to lure you and really it is Hell. (He chuckles.) None of that. It's just so much, you don't even weep about it. That's when your family and your friends show up. When you notice you're not alone.

Me: Who was the first one to meet you?

Erik: Well, hell, I can't even remember.

Me: Was Denise [my sister] there? Aunt Denise. I think she was there to greet you, right?

Erik: Yes. I remember seeing a whole bunch of faces. It's different now. Looking back, I can get the feeling much more clearly, rather than relying on what I was seeing or saying.

Me: Yeah, because, in spirit, it's more about feelings than about mental, brain-based remembering of details. I think that's why people get disappointed when they go to a medium and ask validation questions like, "What did we put in your pocket when we buried you?" You don't remember things like that anymore. It's not important after you cross over. It's all about feelings.

Erik: You're right. And trust me, we're not checking our fucking pockets, either.

Me: Exactly. All right. Let's go on to the life review. What's the life review like? I mean, maybe they're all different, but give me a general idea about what the life review entails.

Erik: Yeah, sometimes you feel like you're going into this room, like an IMAX theater, and it's almost a 360[-degree view], but you get to feel the emotions and impressions that other people perceived of you. So, it's like you're going through this life review and you get to see for yourself, what you've done. You see *yourself* through other people.

Jamie (laughing): I can't imitate that. Basically, he said, "That's totally wrong. That's fucked up. It's the worst joke you could play on anyone."

Me: So, you're like that [other] person. You're seeing through their eyes and feeling what they felt?

Erik: Yes.

Me: Oof. Boy, that's not fun. If, on Earth, you resolved those issues, if you made amends with that person, do you still have to go through that with that person?

Erik: No! No.

Me: Okay, good.

Erik: If it's truly resolved, it's not on your plate.

Me (chuckling): Ooh, I'm going to go around apologizing to a lot of people!

[Jamie and Erik laugh.]

Erik: And the life review is not like somebody comes in and says, "Excuse me. It's time for your life review. It's at 2:30. Please walk into this room and have a seat."

[I chuckle.]

Erik: It just kind of overtakes you, and it's weird. It happens really fast, but you'll feel like you've been in it forever.

Me: Well, what causes the life review? I don't understand. What are its origins? Who decides this? Who creates this?

Erik: Most of the time, it's actually the consciousness, the human experience, the need for the human to do a checklist. Energetically and spiritually, it's not really necessary. You don't need to go through those checkpoints, because, if you came in spiritually, energetically connected, you already know what those checkpoints are. So, you know, this is pretty much for every living person, since we function more from our brain than any other part.

Me: Uh-huh.

Erik: So, it's almost like the brain decompressing, running through everything, but it's in reverse. You get to understand how other people perceived you for you. And your answers are given to you. "Oh! That's why this happened this way!" You put things to rest in a very quick way.

Me: So, is it painful, emotionally?

Erik: Nah. It's definitely fucked up, but it's not painful. You don't leave wrecks like the *Titanic*, right, Mom?

[Jamie and I laugh.]

Me: So, was yours long? Did you have to go through a whole lot?

Erik: No, it wasn't a whole lot. Mine was mostly the voices in my head. You know, my fucked up shit.

Me: What do you mean?

Erik: I had to have conversations with myself quite a bit, you know, to talk myself down from shit and try to understand myself. That's mostly what I came across.

Me: Oh. Who did you have to deal with the most, as far as your life review was concerned?

Erik: Mostly my family.

Me: Yes, of course. Okay. Anything else on the life review?

Erik: Nah. That's probably it.

Me: Do you ever have to go through life reviews for past lives at the same time, or is it only for this current life?

Erik: It's pretty much decompressing the life you are just exiting.

Me: Okay. Now, this white tunnel. This white light you hear about. Of course, some people experience it; some people don't. Why do some experience it and others don't, and what the hell is it?

Erik (teasing): Only the good get to go down the tunnel. No, really. That's bullshit.

Me: It reminds me of that show *The Outer Limits*, where the guys jump into this big swirly circle.

[Jamie laughs.]

Erik: No, really it's based on a belief system.

Me: What is it? Does it exist?

Erik: The tunnel of white light?

Me: Yeah.

Erik: Here's my two cents about it. When you die, if that's what you believed in—that, when you die, you're gonna see this bright white light and all that crap—then I think that's what you're going to get.

Me: Okay.

Erik: But also, the actual death of the brain, the lack of oxygen and everything, creates tunnel vision. Is that the light you go into when you cross into death? No. That's your brain dying.

Me: Well, the belief system had to start from someplace.

Erik: It started from people who had near-death experiences or whatever and their brains were dying, and they got up and talked about it—that they saw God and angels and all this. Consciously—

Jamie (to Erik): Thank you for saying that. This makes sense.

Erik: Consciously, you're trying to look through the eyes that are set in your head, so, when the brain is dying, that's what you're seeing. Intuitively, if you're looking with the third eye, you don't have to see a tunnel of white light to cross over into the Beyond.

Me: Okay.

Erik: So, if you're looking with your third eye—the intuitive eye—most likely it'll be like going into another room.

Me: Yeah, a lot of people describe it that way—like going into another room. When you got pulled back by your shoulders, where'd you end up?

Erik (chuckling): In another room!

Me: Okay, and—

Erik: It's wild. The room around me just kind of disappeared. Where I was just dissolved. I think that's the only way I know how to say it. Dim the lights. Turn the lights on. You're in a different space. There's nothing fast about it. It wasn't like a quick jerk or anything. It was more of how you feel your body going to sleep. It's more like that.

Me: I remember when you were doing your life review, you talked about how you sat at a long table and you had your head in your hands.

Erik: Uh-huh.

Me: All right. We went backward there. What were some of the adjustments you had to make when you crossed over? What were some of the most, uh, I won't say "difficult" . . . The most interesting. The most intense.

Erik: How to move.

Me: How to move! Yeah. "I cain't feel my laigs!"

Jamie: He's laughing.

Me: That's from the movie *Major Payne.* "That's 'cause they ain't there!"

Jamie (laughing): I have no idea what you're talking about, but he's almost on the floor!

Me: 'Cause we watched it all the time. It was with one of the Wayans brothers. It's so funny. Erik loved it.

[Jamie is still laughing.]

Erik: Similar to that, but it's just interesting. I'd say that's the most urgent one that you come across.

Me: Uh-huh.

Erik: You know, how to get from here to there. And it's weird, because you keep moving and traveling, yet you can't explain to yourself how you're doing it. It's like, "What's happening. Oh shit, it's happening!" You don't know how.

Me: Was it scary?

Erik (chuckling): No. No, I wasn't afraid, but I definitely wasn't getting all the answers I needed ASAP, so that was weird.

Me: Was there some sort of guide who was there for you during your death, your life review, or afterward? Wasn't there anybody to help you?

Erik (laughing): If there was, that dick must have been hiding behind the curtain, because I didn't see anyone!

Me: Oh, my God! That's awful. How come? Was it because you didn't ask for help?

Erik: Oh, I didn't ask for help.

[Typical guy. They won't ask for directions.]

Erik: And I think I just wanted to be alone.

Me: Do you think that, if you had asked for help, somebody would have come?

Erik: Oh, yeah, with bells a-ringing.

Me: Why did you want to be alone?

Erik: 'Cause I wanted rest.

Me: Was part of it shame? Did you think you'd get in trouble for doing what you did?

Erik: Wow. That's interesting.

[Pause]

Me: Like, "Uh-oh. I'm busted. Don't take me to Hell!"

Erik: No.

Me: Okay. That's good.

Erik (amazed): Nah, I never felt like that! How cool is that?

Me: That's awesome. So, you couldn't move. Tell me about the whole experience of learning how to move.

Erik: Well, it's like I consciously couldn't make myself go, but if I thought about being somewhere, I'd end up there. It kept happening, but I couldn't figure out how exactly it was happening.

Me: Could you see your arms and legs?

[Pause]

Me: Or were you just consciousness? Could you see your spirit body?

Erik: Yeah. That's mostly what you see. You don't see yourself like you were as a human.

Me: So, it wasn't like you were seeing only your environment, like you were just an awareness of self without a body?

Erik: Yeah, without a human body. I had an energetic shape, you know, as light, and I felt like myself. I knew my whereabouts. I knew what had happened. It's not like I was thrown into some strange world without a map. I felt like I belonged and I was safe. I was never afraid, but it was just the smallest things like that that would fuck you in the head a little bit.

Me: But when you looked down, you could see your legs and your feet and all that? It wasn't a human body, but you weren't just like a ball of light?

Erik: Correct. Yeah, right. I had an energetic shape like my human body.

Me: And you could move? You could look at your hand and make a fist, move your legs and things like that?

Erik: Oh, yeah!

Me: So, it was more about moving from one place to another.

Erik: Yeah.

Me: So, you learned how to think of a place and be there?

Erik: Yeah.

Me: What were some other adjustments that you had to make when you crossed over?

Erik: Well, I was used to kind of arguing with myself in my head or having contradictory thoughts and emotions, but that shit just doesn't happen. That was weird.

Me: Hmm. What happens instead?

Erik (slightly frustrated): I don't really know how to explain it. You just don't have them. You couldn't be angry and happy.

Me: So, more peace. No more conflict in your head.

Erik: Yes.

Me: How old were you when you had no conflict in your head?

Erik: I had moments of it, but never consistently.

Me: Well, I don't think anybody has it consistently.

Erik: Really?

Me: Where they're always, always, always at peace, with no conflict in their head? Of course not.

Erik: C'mon. There's gotta be people. Isn't that what being happy is?

Me: One hundred percent of the time?

Jamie (to Erik): Yeah, Erik. There's—

Me: C'mon! What if someone is super constipated, and they're sitting there on the toilet, and they can't pinch one off? That is *not* a happy situation!

Erik (chuckling): Yeah, but that's a physical conflict.

Me: It doesn't make any difference. It's going to create some emotional conflict. Nobody is totally at peace all the time unless they're the Dalai Lama.

Erik: You must have an issue with shit, Mom.

Me: Look at you and your scatological humor! I wouldn't talk! Okay. Let's move on. What are some other adjustments you had to make? Any others?

Erik: Those two are the main ones.

Me: At what point did you ask for help? When did you finally say, "I need help"?

Erik: When I wanted to get back to my family and I didn't know how.

Me: Aw. Did you miss us?

Erik: Yeah!

Me: So, who appeared?

Jamie: This was a female guide. Not his aunt. This was someone who was telling him how to cross dimensions and how to communicate.

Erik: About this time, it was when you were doing all the research and trying to find mediums, you know. So, I was trying to learn how to talk through them and get into it. By then, I didn't have any conflict with my emotions. I was perfectly A-okay. I knew how to travel, and then I immediately started learning how to communicate to humans. Cross-dimensional communication.

Me: How did you ask? Did you just think, "I need help!"?

Erik: Yeah. Yeah.

Me: Or did you get on the loudspeaker and yell, "A little help here!"

Erik: No, I thought about it. I would need someone to come teach me, and that's all you do. You just think that.

Me: Did you have to go through some sort of therapy? They say some people have to go through therapy to mend energetically, and so on. Did you go through that process, too?

Erik: I did some, yeah.

Me: One medium told me that you had to go through a lot less therapy than most suicides.

Erik: Yeah.

Me: Why is that?

Erik: Because it was the spiritual contract I'd written for this life, it was the end of my line, whereas, with most people who take their lives, it's not the end of their line. They're just doing it out of revenge, or because they want an out or avoidance.

Me: Okay. It's not an exit point for them.

Erik: Yes.

Me: All right. Now, what do most spirits miss about the earthly plane. I know you have all of your buddies over there, and they're like, "Oh, my God, I really miss pizza" or whatever, but what do most, if you were to do a survey, miss about the earthly plane?

Erik: Food, number one. Sex, number two.

[Jamie giggles.]

Me: But I thought the sex was better over there.

Erik: It is, but it's not physical like that. It's different. So different.

Me: And why do you miss food? Can't you conjure up the taste and texture, or is it different?

Erik: It's totally different.

Me: But can't you create that taste, the texture, and the fullness in the belly?

Erik: It's the whole chewing it, smelling it, waiting for it to be done. I mean, we don't really have that kind of process. We don't need it.

Me: Yeah, but can't you create every aspect of it like you've described?

Erik: It's not the same, Mom.

Me: It's not the same.

Erik: It's like artificial flavor is not the same as the real thing.

Me: I see. And sex is not quite, uh . . . you don't have that physical, the physical body.

[Jamie bursts out in laughter.]

Jamie: Uh-huh. He's talking about the "bang banging."

Me: Oh, God, Erik. Well, you didn't have much of it when you were here, poor guy. I guess you'll have to come back as a prostitute.

[Jamie laughs hard.]

Me: Or, what do you call it? A gigolo. Come back as a gigolo.

Erik: If I come back, I'm definitely coming back with a dick.

Me: So, come back as a gigolo and then you can really get some—on a regular basis.

[Jamie still hasn't stopped laughing.]

Erik: Jamie has just checked out!

[We all can't help but laugh at that one.]

Me: Okay. Let's talk about this: when spirits cross back over, what do they miss about Heaven?

Erik: Huh?

Me: When they come back to Heaven and say, "I'm so glad to be back because I missed . . ." What do they miss about Heaven?

Erik: The bullshit.

Me: You miss getting away from the bullshit.

Erik: Yeah. The emotional conflict. That's why a lot of spirits like to come to Earth—to feel the lower vibrational emotions. Hardship. Struggle.

Me: But when they come back to Heaven, they go, "Ugh, I miss those emotional conflicts."

Jamie: Does that make sense? 'Cause the way he's explaining it is that they're attracted to it, so that's why they reincarnate. That's where some of the deeper lessons are learned.

Me: Uh-huh.

Erik: Through the conflict. There's no conflict in Heaven or Home. So, when the human dies and becomes a spirit again, the ease of life is sometimes shocking and hard to adjust to.

Me: Yeah.

Erik: 'Cause they just spent all that time adjusting to conflict.

Jamie: Oh. So he's saying not that they miss that the most. It's just that it's the hardest to adapt to.

Me: To not have the conflict anymore? You like the conflict-free dimension, but it's hard to adapt to. But I want to know what they miss about Heaven when they come back. "Oh, my God, I'm so glad to be back, because I miss . . ."

Jamie: Glad to be back on Earth or glad to be back in Heaven?

Me: In Heaven.

[Why is this so damn hard?]

Erik: Oh, the ease of life. Peace. Love. Unconditional love.

Me: All right. [finally!] What are the coolest new abilities you gained that you didn't have on Earth?

Jamie: Coolest new abilities.

Me: Yeah.

Jamie (to Erik): That aren't raunchy!

Me: Really!

[Jamie giggles.]

Me: I didn't expect we could go there on *this* question, but leave it to Erik.

Erik: Telepathy. Love it. It's accurate. It's better than instant messages. It's better than text. It's better than email.

[No fax?]

Me: Okay. What else?

Erik: Not being stuck on planet Earth. You can just go wherever the "F" you wanna go.

Me: Why are you saying, "F"? Seriously, Jamie!

Jamie: I know! He said, "You can just go wherever the fuck you wanna go."

Me: There we go!

[Jamie laughs.]

Me: He's got you all messed up today.

Jamie: Oh, the highs and lows we've gone through already!

Me: I swear to god! This is Emotional Roller-Coaster Day. Okay, what else? I can imagine the frequent flyer miles you can rack up there!

Jamie: Now that! He loves that!

Me: What else. Name a couple more.

Erik: A couple more. Transcending space and time. Time travel. Going back into your past lives. Oh, what about going to the fucking library?

Me: The Akashic Records?

Erik: Yeah. That shit fucking blows your mind.

Me: Tell me about it.

Erik: I can't even plan how to get to the grocery store and buy everything that I need, and I go into [the library] and all my past lives, my future lives, my now lives, my afterlife lives are all finely tuned. How the fuck does that happen?

Me: What? Do you go into a library and open up a book? I mean, what's it like?

Erik: No, it's not really like a book. It's more like a never-ending page. It's not like a "lick, flip" book.

[I chuckle.]

Erik: It's kind of like a scroll, in a way, like one constant page, but you don't have to manually unroll it. The information just comes to you.

Me: Is it like a holographic display?

Erik: Sort of like that. Yeah, yeah, yeah. It's technologically advanced.

Me: Do you just take your thumb and scroll through it like an iPhone, or do you think about going to the next life or whatever?

Erik: Yep. It shows you what you want it to show you.

Me: Interesting. Does it have cool colors? Glowing? Sparkly?

Erik: Yeah. To me, I see it in a kind of glowing blue color.

Me: Hmm. I can almost see it. Probably have.

After this session with Jamie, I felt that she and Erik had a definite connection. In this and future sessions, they enjoy a sweet and playful banter that was and is infectious and loving. Erik has said that he likes the way Jamie communicates because she doesn't "take it so heavy." The two of them often behave a lot like siblings, equal parts pestering and affectionate.

Erik's Life Review

As Erik mentioned in the session about his experiences directly after death (above), he went through what he called a "life review" shortly after he left his body. Below, he tells me a little more about what that means and what it was like for him.

Me: Can you share some details about your life review with us, Erik?

Erik: Well, there was this big table where everybody was going to sit down, like at a family dinner. There was a lot of music; there was a lot of laughing. Oh, and Mom, I asked four souls from your soul group, who aren't part of your life now, if they could help you through all this. I want to do something to help the family. I want to be able to do something for you guys. If there is anything at all I can do to help anyone in the family, please let me know, and I'll do everything I can. I want to feel like I'm still part of the family. Ask me to do stuff. I can't exactly take out the garbage, but—

Me (chuckling): I'll get a chore list together for you!

Erik (laughing): Mom, you're going to notice that things have been done, and you'll ask other people, "Did you do that?" or "Did you do this?" They'll say "no," and you'll know it was me!

[I found that so comforting. Proof of Erik's presence was crucial to me as I adjusted to our new relationship.]

Me (prodding gently): Okay, let's get back to what happened next.

[Erik was always easily distracted, just like his mom.]

Erik: Oh, yeah, right. Well, I was at this big long table, and I felt dazed. I was still euphoric, but I was dazed. It's like one minute I was in my physical body and the next minute I was a free spirit without physical limitations, and I kept asking, "I'm really a spirit, right? I mean, I don't get to go back to that lifetime; I've let that lifetime go, right?" And they assured me that I had.

Then I started "the review." Nobody did the review but me. I was sitting at the table alone. Uh, I was sitting there, and everyone was talking about how happy they were that I'm back. No matter how we pass, we're always welcomed back with open arms. Everyone is always thrilled to see us again. Anyway, so I'm sitting at the table, and I've got my elbows on top of it. I've got my head in my hands, and I'm reviewing my life. I started sobbing when I remembered being a little boy, and you calling me your "little man" and doing things with me and telling me what a big man I was gonna be. I've taken all of that away. Those were the worst moments of the review. I want to thank Pappa for treating me like an adult. Pappa, you treated me like an adult for as long as I can remember. That meant a lot to me.

So I finished my review, and I considered what I could have done but didn't, and what I did do but shouldn't have. I don't know how long the review took. I didn't mark time. No one here marks time. But it didn't take long, because the candles were still burning on my cake—my "welcome home" cake. Then I felt this heaviness, this really emotional heaviness. I was approached by a female soul who offered to counsel me; she offered me therapy. So I've been going to what I guess you'd call therapy. She's not only helping me understand why I did it—why I took my life—but how I can go back to the earthly plane with the healing I was supposed to do this lifetime, without killing myself again. Wow, Mom, if I could have seen what I was healing from in past lives—no wonder I was so fucking depressed and angry. No wonder, Mom!

Erik's New Experiences as an Untethered Soul

Erik's loquaciousness and willingness to share his experiences beyond the veil as a newly untethered soul are not limited to his relationship with Jamie. On the contrary, in this next conversation, Erik describes in detail what things are like without his body. He tells this story through Kim, the first translator we worked with.

Erik: I want you to let other people know that we have lots of company here. A lot of parents who have lost kids worry that their kid is all alone, but it's not that way. Plus, we can manifest anything we want. We imagine what we want to eat, and it's right there. We live where we want; we live how we want. We don't feel hot or cold. Thought creates reality much faster here. It happens in an instant.

Me: Erik, I'd like to know how you have such powerful control over your [spiritual] energy; you passed such a short time ago!

Erik: I don't know. I really don't know. I guess it's due to my level of enlightenment. I've got a very high level of enlightenment. You guys know that. Mom, you especially know that. You're the best mom anyone could ever have. We've talked more after I died than we did in the last couple of years [I was alive], haven't we? . . . Everybody's been kinda surprised over here that I did what I did and then I didn't have that much to heal. I really didn't have that much to heal. I never will go through all of this again. I've let go of loss. The depression was like a secondary issue for me. It was mostly confusion and the sense of loss and the sense of hopelessness, and now that's all gone. All that healing has been done from past lifetimes. I figure I have one more lifetime to go, that's it. One more.

[At that moment, I felt such an overwhelming pride for my son and his mounting accomplishments as a spiritual being, I had to share those feelings with him.]

Me: I've always tried to teach you, Erik, that doing things for other people feels so good, and I'm so proud that you've learned that, or you're realizing that, on the spiritual plane. You've accomplished so much in such a short time. The fact that you feel like you didn't accomplish that much here on Earth really makes no difference when you're accomplishing so much where you are now. Plus, Erik, you accomplished a lot more than you think while you were here on the earthly plane, because you gave so much love to so many. You taught people to love; you taught people humility; you taught people to live in the moment. So, I'm really proud of you, Erik.

Erik: Thanks, Mom! Now I realize how much I contributed and how much I did. I'm still trying to get to the bottom of why I felt so worthless. I know part of it is from past lifetimes; I know it, I know it. But I don't get why I couldn't pull myself out of that black hole; why I chose to end my earthly life without having more positive or optimistic thoughts about the next moment or the next hour or the next day; and why I didn't just come to you and say, "Mom, I'm really, really, really fucked up; I need your help." I know you would have helped me.

Me: Erik, maybe you knew deep inside that you would accomplish more in the spiritual plane.

Erik: Well, that's the way it's turning out. Exactly! I feel confident. I feel certain that if I had stayed there, I would have continued to question my worth and what I was contributing, and that would have made me useless. Mom, you're absolutely right, as usual! You see what no one else does!

[Then, Erik abruptly changed the subject, moving on to something he obviously felt like sharing. I could feel the pent-up excitement.]

Erik (proudly): Oh, yeah, I just got a boat! I just got my own place here, Mom. It's like a condo. It's my bachelor pad.

Me: So, [is your new life] similar to the one you had on Earth?

Erik: Yeah, we can have everything we had on Earth. We can go out for pizza, have relationships, get married; it's just the same, but we can manifest everything so much faster. Plus, we don't have the issues we did on the earthly plane. We have our life's work as souls, we travel, and we can have children. I have my own bachelor pad. It's at the beach, but by the beach there's a loch or fjord where I take my boat. I've created a place for myself that looks a lot like Norway, and I love it! [Kim says he is showing her his place, and she starts giggling.]

Kim: It's sort of what you'd expect for a bachelor. He has a leather couch and a big flat-screen television; an end table with a lamp; a bed; and a bigger lamp next to the couch. That's it! It's pretty sparse! (To Erik:) No table? Where do you eat?

[We'll go into why some spirits enjoy "eating" and manifesting material comforts they had on Earth later.]

Erik: On the couch in front of the television, of course!

Me: So, I'm curious. Can you communicate with us even when you're not in the same place we are? In other words, can you and I talk even when I'm at home and you're somewhere else?

Erik: Of course!

Me: Can you hear me when I call for you? Can you hear me talk to you in my head?

Erik: Absolutely! I hear everything you say and think. Mom, it's just like I was still on the earthly plane, when we were communicating even if we weren't speaking. It's exactly the same thing. Say I was at school or at the shop or out riding. We often communicated with each other without saying a thing, and when we were together, we finished each other's sentences. It's exactly the same thing. I hear everything you say, and now I listen! [Kim shares that Erik is laughing at this last remark.]

Me: Do you eavesdrop [on us] sometimes?

Erik: Of course I eavesdrop!

Me (giggling): What a nosy boy!

Erik: Anyone in spirit form knows what you on the earthly plane say. We not only eavesdrop on what you say, but on what you think and feel!

Me: Oh, good. Maybe you can make sense of some of the things that go on in my head! Now, do you ever get frustrated with us when we don't pick up on you? It must be really difficult sometimes.

Erik (chuckling): To answer your other question about making sense of what you're thinking—not on my best day!

Me (laughing hard): I know, that's next to impossible! [Kim asks me to repeat my previous question, and I do.]

Erik: No, I'm not frustrated; I'm just resigned. I know that if I speak louder and make myself more tangible with my new electrical energy, then you'll know I'm there. I've talked about this with my new friends here on the spiritual plane, and they're like, "This person doesn't pick up on me, and I talk, talk, talk for nothing." So, I say, "Well, I think what you need to do is try to make yourself more tangible; make yourself be seen and heard more tangibly, and then that's gonna change things." See, Mom? Look how much more you're picking up on me lately! And I know your ability to perceive and communicate with me will only get stronger. It's mostly up to us over here to make our presence known, though.

Me: And us over here to be more receptive.

Erik: Mom, that's a good point; that's true. I have some friends here in spirit who materialize and really make their presence known, and the family members are in too much pain to be able to notice them. You're right, Mom; you're exactly right. So it takes strength over here for us to materialize, and it takes courage for you to pick up on us.

Me: Do you and other spirits experience emotions?

Erik: Shit, yeah! We don't have the same issues anymore, but we all have personalities and emotions.

Me: So, can you still get sad?

Erik: Oh, yeah. Oh, you can get fucked up over here too!

Me: Does it make you unhappy when you see us sad or when you hear our thoughts of grief?

Erik: Yes.

Me (eager for a more comforting explanation): Do you look at us grieving and think, "Hey, you guys have blinders on; you don't even know the half of it. When you come over here, you'll see there's no such thing as true loss"?

Erik: No, no, no. That's not it at all, Mom. There is true loss. There's loss when a human being you're close to passes away, and there's loss when you're here where I am and your loved ones go back to Earth.

Me: I never thought about that. But the loss is never permanent, right?

Erik: Of course not. We just miss them until we're together again. When I see you expressing sadness and grief, I understand it perfectly. I take full, 100 percent responsibility for it. I know that, if I hadn't committed suicide, I would still be there—at worst, frustrating you—instead of creating this great grief. Every time someone expresses grief over losing me, I feel totally responsible, and I understand it perfectly. You're all entitled [to your grief].

Me: Well, I just don't want you to feel so uncomfortable that you stay away because it's too painful for you!

Erik (laughing): Mom, don't be stupid!

Kim: You know, his sense of humor is so amazing.

Me: I know; he's always had a great sense of humor. (To Erik:) Erik, I want you to know that I am happy for you, because I sense that you are happier where you are now.

Erik: I am, Mom. I've never been happier.

Me (struggling to choke back my tears): And I've been telling you this lately. I may grieve, because I long to hold you—my baby—in my arms, but I am happy that you've found peace and joy, and I know we'll be together again someday.

Erik: Thank you, Mom.

Me: Erik, let me ask you this: You know how you said that when you popped out of your body, you felt this expanded knowingness—this broader perspective—and you saw people for who they really are?

What did you mean by that? For example, what did you see when you saw me for who I really am?

Erik: Now, I heard a couple of questions there, Mom. First of all, when a soul pops out of a human body, you can immediately see people for who and what they are—meaning you can see their exact level of enlightenment, what their potential is, what they've done in past lifetimes, who they've been, what they've achieved, what they've contributed. You have a perfect understanding of their personality and the life you shared with them. So, Mom, when my soul popped out of my body, and I looked at you, I saw a soul who is at a pinnacle of enlightenment. I saw someone who is totally nurturing, understanding, inspiring, motivating, supportive, encouraging, loving, generous, giving, and funny. [Not terribly comfortable with flattery, I blush.] I could remember all of your past lifetimes, all the lifetimes we shared together. Hey, Mom, you know what we've done? When we met here [before], you and I would sometimes go visit other planets together!

Me: Cool! We'll do it again, I promise.

Erik: I'm waiting for you, but I know it's going to be a long, long time from your perspective. But that's good; that's okay.

Me: Yes, I understand. Do you think you're usually more comfortable in the spiritual plane than in the physical plane, Erik? I feel that I am.

Erik: Yes, being in the physical plane was like being in pain all the time, like with a migraine or an abscess. I found some peace in Norway, but all the peace I found was fleeting. That's why I always jumped from one thing to the next, to the next, to the next. That's why I didn't stick with anything long-term. The pleasure or enjoyment or stimulation it gave me was always so fleeting. I would start feeling pain again, and then I'd jump to something else.

Me: Well, I'm glad you're having a good time there, sweetie. I'm so glad you're happy. That's all a mother dreams of—that her child finds joy and fulfillment in life.

Erik's visits—especially his mischievous pranks—and these first precious conversations we had with each other through both Kim and Jamie, began to bring me some peace of mind and hope as a mother who had just lost a child. Although Erik's description of his own death left me reeling, I was relieved and happy to see that his humor had not changed. I felt he was indeed "my Erik." Not only that, he was the Erik I remembered before he plunged into that dark depression as a teen, which led him to the desperate measures he took to end his pain. He truly seemed happy. As I adjusted to all of the ways Erik had begun to communicate with us, I developed a tentative hypothesis surrounding my son's existence as an untethered soul. Namely, I realized that my son had to "live" somewhere in the afterlife, but I couldn't yet put words to what this could mean.

I continued to tread this unfamiliar territory of the afterlife with the help of trusted spiritual communicators, my family and friends, and of course, Erik himself. My first miles down this road were filled with caution and hesitation, but there was so much I wanted to know, especially about what it was really like to exist in the afterlife and what "the afterlife" actually meant. As I mentioned above, I had developed a theory that my son "lives" somewhere, but what was that "somewhere" really like? How was he emotionally? How did he spend his time? How is his "life" different since his death? Above all, I had a powerful need to continue some sort of relationship with Erik, if such a thing were possible. In our following conversations, my questions and more were answered, and our new relationship began to gain its footing.

PART II

THE UNTETHERED SOUL

Many of us cringe at the thought of our own mortality. It's very human. For some, death is a shadow that hangs over us, and we anticipate that ill-timed moment when a bus will mow us down, an artery will get clogged, or a cancer cell will materialize and grow in the sacred garden that is our body. Sometimes, one feels that the threshold into the unknown is far away, and other times, one feels that one foot is in the grave and the other's on a banana peel. Whatever your feelings are about your own mortality, I invite you to hang on tight for this eye-opening ride through it all, as narrated by our tour guide, Erik, in the following conversations about what death is actually like, what souls can do and accomplish, and the real nature of the afterlife itself, among many other fascinating topics.

5

ERIK DESCRIBES
DEATH IN GENERAL

Erik kicks off our discussion on death in classic Erik style—with a prank and a laugh. Before each session, Erik often pops in before I call and rattles Jamie with his mischief.

Jamie: So, yesterday I was doing a reading for a woman, and I kept smelling fish. I mean, like, really fishy fish, stinky old fish.

Me: Eww! Old fish? That's the worst!

Jamie: And I kept stopping the reading and looking at the woman, like, you know, [is there something I should be picking up on] related to fish? I couldn't really figure it out at all! I still couldn't figure it out when she left! Well, do you know who it was who was doing that?

Me (laughing): Oh, I can only guess.

Jamie: It didn't even dawn on me. It didn't even cross my mind.

Me: He's very playful. I mean, I don't know whether you read the blog, but no member is safe from that mischief-maker!

Jamie: Oh, my goodness! He has been keeping himself busy! And he's here and wide awake.

Me: Hi, Erik!

[Jamie giggles.]

Erik: Hi, Mom.

Me: Okay, Erik, what would you like to share about death in general? It's a fear-laden topic in the hearts and minds of many.

Jamie (chuckling): He's kind of rubbing his chin.

Erik: Can we come up with another word for "death"?

Me: "Transition"? I don't know! You tell me; you're the expert!

Erik: Death is just like birth. We "birth in" to this amazing world, and then we "birth in" to another world, the world that I'm a part of now.

Me: Which do you think is more difficult?

Erik: Oh, definitely being born into the human form.

Me: And what about transitioning to where you are now, Erik?

Jamie: He takes a deep breath.

Erik: [It's like] going home. Well, because of *you* and the blog members, I've had a lot of interactions with other spirits who've talked about death—their death. Their transition. It's all very different for everyone. I really believe—

Jamie: He's pausing to think, and his eyes are scrunched.

Erik: Mom, it's like this: Everyone has such a different experience, and I really think it's meant to be that way so that we can learn and experience what we're capable of dealing with. Most of the time, when I talk to spirits, even if they were in an immense amount of pain when they died, they don't really recall it as vividly as you recall painful things as a human. There's just not a big emotional attachment to it. But most of the time, death is painless unless the spirit wants to experience a painful death in order to grow. We usually grow best through hardships and challenges. Oh, and something else about pain during and after transition: Pain is related to the physical body, and we're not in it anymore. We don't have those body memories. Those old scars, those old pains and strains, are gone. We're set free from them. We have that pain when we're in the body, but as soon as we're released—

Jamie: He's giving me this really funny image of a horse race, when the gate is opened and the horse just dashes out like, "Oh, yay! Get me outta here!" [Jamie and I both laugh.]

Erik: Yeah. That's when we really begin to run the race. Everything is faster and freer, less limiting and cramped.

Me: Okay. Now, I know that a lot of people who have had NDEs [near-death experiences] talk about going toward a light and going through a tunnel. I know you said everyone has a different experience, but are there some things that are constant?

Erik: It's all based on their belief system. What I find most profound is what happens to children when they die, because they really don't have a belief system yet. They don't have that training or indoctrination. They cross over to here and—

Jamie: Oops, now he's changing topic. [We both sigh knowingly.]

Erik: You know, I was talking the other day to somebody . . . So I was talking to him about—

Jamie (giggling): Slow down, Erik! Take a breath.

Me: He can talk a mile a minute, that boy!

[There's a pause while Jamie catches up with Erik, then she paraphrases what he says.]

Jamie: He was talking to this other gentleman about the structures of the brain. And he says there's been a lot of research about [what happens] when the brain dies. Apparently, there are two minutes afterward, in which the cells die and there is no oxygen; and an image is perceived as a light, and it has a tunnel effect. And he says you can read all these articles from scientists claiming that's exactly what the tunnel effect is.

Erik: Well, I gotta give it some credit. Not all though.

Jamie: He's shaking his head like he's saying, "Oh, no way, not all!"

Erik: But I do think this is the way our bodies work to comfort us. I've been told that [our bodies are] designed this way, because it is the natural progression of death, of body, and of spirit.

Me: Okay.

Erik: Why wouldn't our brains start us off on this new journey while it dies? It just makes so much friggin' sense to me.

Jamie: I've never thought about that before!

Me: Interesting. I've read the research you're talking about, Erik. It has to do with the lack of oxygen to the occipital lobe of the brain. Okay, now I'd like to go back to children if we can. Tell me how [they experience death].

Erik: Get this: Children with no belief system—what do you think they report when they have NDEs?

Me: I don't know; I give up.

Erik: The purest of pure things. They see the light. They go into the light, and in this light, they see people. Mom, they're so little, they don't know that it's, you know, Grandpa Joe or Great-Grandma Suzy, for example. But the child knows that these people love them. They have an experience like that.

[Long pause, followed by Jamie laughing.]

Jamie (still giggling): Okay. You gotta go back, Erik. Back up a little for me. He's talking about people who believe they've had NDEs, but when they die and come back, they talk about a council of white-robed people, and people with Roman togas and wraps, and you know, streets lined with gold.

Erik: Mom, I know that's in our belief system, but that's exactly what it is. It's a man creating a story, passing it down.

Me: Oh, yeah. Okay.

Erik: And since the togas have status and most feel like the monks are very connected with God, we imagine that our spirit guides dress like monks or leaders of that era.

Me: So, do we create that design, or do they create it for us so that we'll be more comfortable and better oriented when we pass over?

Erik: Oh, no, we create that for ourselves. Our beliefs are the strongest fence that we have around us. It can keep things in, and it can keep things out.

Me: What about skeptics or atheists who don't believe in an afterlife? What happens when they die?

Jamie (laughing): He's got that "cat who ate the canary" smile again!

Me: Oh, my gosh, I can just see it right now in my mind!

Erik: Well, they want to go into nothingness—or at least that's what they believe will happen—so they do! And then, they have a thought and they realize they're having a thought. That curiosity right there sparks them into exploring the space they're actually in. When they begin to do that, they transition to what I call "home."

Me: What happens if they don't explore? Do they float around in nothingness for all eternity?

Erik: There are spirits who come to rescue them and orient them, but the rescuers have to wait until the person's energy vibration opens up and gets higher.

Me: What about people who believe in Hell and think they belong there?

Erik: Then they have no opportunity to see the light and cross over. They have to wait until their vibration goes up. Eventually, it does. It always does. Really, Hell is just a name for the separation from the light. Mom, we who believe in [a higher power] know that it's in everything. So how can we ever be separate from it?

Jamie (laughing): I love his mannerisms!

Me: I know; he has a lot of funny ones!

Jamie (still laughing): When he gets deep and is thinking, boy, his body really moves into it!

Erik: Mom, it doesn't make sense! The light is omnipresent, so Hell can't exist. If the light is everything—every being, every universe, every dimension—how can something like Hell exist? It's impossible.

Me: So, what do people do when they think they should be in Hell? Do they imagine Hell and create their own personal reality of Hell?

Erik: Well, what I've seen happen—

Jamie: He sits back now.

Erik: Let's take the Baptists, for example. You know they believe they have to go through Hell before they reach God. They believe they have to face their demons—the evil that resides inside of them—to purify themselves. So, people with those strong beliefs, they don't feel the light right away. They see their fear, the fear of mankind, all of the lower energy—and they fight. They have that struggle, and then they get into the light, and they feel they've survived. Is it necessary? I don't think so, but that's their belief and their choice.

Me: So, in your case, Erik, it wasn't a big surprise when you died and experienced what you experienced, because your belief system was kind of our belief system, a more spiritual one, though not necessarily one of organized religions. As a family, we explored different options. Did this make your transition a bit easier?

Erik: Oh, yeah. I have to thank you for that. I think it's so weird that people can be so careless and carefree with their lives because they think death will rescue them, or that, when they die, all will be forgiven. Little do they know, their afterlife is based on the beliefs they create while they're alive.

Me: Their whole afterlife? Really?

Erik: Yes, 'cause if they believe that this is all they get, then their perspective is going to be very narrow. So, that's all they will get. It's the same in life. Haven't you realized?

Jamie (giggling): Beans, Erik? All right. He says, maybe you've never tried beans, and then at age thirty, you try beans. Then all of a sudden, that's all you can see everywhere: beans, beans, beans. That's because you're more open to it.

Me (chuckling): Well, if they're green beans, you've probably never tried them, Erik!

Erik (laughing): That's not true! You made me take some bites!

Me: Well, that's true. You got me there. So, that's really interesting. I remember that, every time I was pregnant, it seemed like every other woman around me was too. So, what you're saying is that the beliefs you have all throughout your life set the foundation for what your death and afterlife experience is?

Erik: Yes.

Me: I know death is different for each person, but as a general rule, what do most souls notice right away?

Erik: Their bodies.

Me: You see your body? That's the first thing you notice?

Erik: No. The body—the way it feels. It's crazy, Mom, because you don't experience any pain, but sometimes that doesn't register until, like, days or weeks later, as Earth time goes. There's no hunger or thirst. You're never too cold or too hot. And some notice it right away. But for others, it's a few days before they go, "Hey, I don't have any pain!" Some people lived with pain for so long, they don't realize when it's gone.

Me: Interesting. So, what else? What other sensations do you notice right away?

Erik: Expansion. You feel expanded and lighter. It's like you're not cramped into that tight space anymore, and you can fill any space you want. Also, one of the first things you notice is that, when you think of something—when you have a thought—you don't get in a car and travel somewhere to see it or go get it. You just end up there. Like, when I think of you, I'm there. When I think of Bestefar in Norway, I'm there.

Me: Yes, you said thought creates reality much faster there—like instantaneously.

Erik (laughing): Oh, yeah!

Me: Must save on those plane tickets. No frequent flyer miles for you, huh, Erik? [Erik laughs.]

Me: But can you create a car or motorcycle or boat, and travel that way if you want to? I know you mentioned that you have a boat, and that you live in your bachelor pad.

Erik: Yeah! Hell, yeah! You can create anything, just like humans can create houses and build their cars. We have the same capabilities here, but it's done in a much different way: easier and quicker.

Jamie (laughing): He's giving me this look like, "Oh, poor you!"

Me: Us poor folks down here have to do everything the hard way, huh?

[Jamie laughs.]

Me: What about the body? After you leave the physical body and look down at your spirit self, do you still have a body of some sort, like a "memory body"? Does your form seem solid to you, at least at first?

Erik: Yes, it does, but I didn't even think about it right after I saw my body. Now I know I can create whatever form I want and be however solid I want to be. I can look like any age; I can wear any clothes; I can be a beam or ball of light; I can be translucent or solid. It's up to me, and I usually change it up depending on who I'm with, whether it's a friend over here or someone human on the earthly plane.

Me: What else do you want to share about death and the moment right after death? You know, what the soul realizes right after death?

Erik: Well, definitely lack of pain, like I said. Ease of movement. How thought creates reality in an instant. Also, these wonderful things are happening to you. There's this full-on weakness that you have at first. For me, I relate that to the whole "I don't know how to maneuver this body" thing I sometimes felt when I was alive. Also, when I had a body on Earth, I would reach out, grab the can, open it up, and drink it. I could feel thirst and take care of it. If I wanted to see my family, I could call or come over or email. But now these patterns that I learned don't exist anymore. They don't work the same way. In the beginning, there's a sense of helplessness. I've heard some spirits call it "release," but you have to sorta relearn how to interact with people and stuff. Some spirits know how to do it right away. You know, entering a dream or moving something away or making something appear. But some of us just take longer before we are able to do certain things.

Me: To do what exactly? Can you give me an example of something you tried to do and it was difficult?

Erik: Like picking up the gun right after I died, remember? Or trying to move my face. My hand went right through those things. Now, I've learned to lower the vibrational frequency of my hands so I can move solid objects on the earthly plane.

From this exchange, I learned that everyone's afterlife is different based on the belief system from our childhood—influenced by our parents, teachers, and peers. I also learned that every spirit has a unique transition and adjustment from life in a physical body on the earthly plane to life as an untethered soul in the spirit realm.

Next, Erik shares how each spirit revisits their life on Earth in order to glean the valuable lessons the human experience holds.

6

THE LIFE REVIEW IN GENERAL

Many who have had near-death experiences recount something they call "the life review," just as Erik did. Each person's experience is a bit different from those of other people, but certain elements are the same. Here, Erik shares what often happens just before and during that process.

Me: Can you tell us more about the life review, in general terms?

Erik: Yeah. Really, that whole "life flashes before your eyes" thing? I got it. You get it. Everyone gets it. Sometimes it happens right at the moment of death. Commonly, if you're getting it right away, that means you're going to get right back into your body.

Me: Oh, really?

Erik: Yeah, 'cause that's the whole big, "Wow! Holy shit! Look what just happened! My life flashed before me; now I know how I want to be; now I know who I want to be. I better go back and make some changes to my life."

Me: Like with near-death experiences! I see that same thing happening in those NDE accounts. They immediately go through the life review.

Erik: Yeah. That's a really powerful kick in the ass; but if you're expected, if you know you're arriving and that this is it, often you're greeted by family, and then the life review begins to happen after that. When I had mine, it was like I was in everybody else's body, looking at myself. I felt what the people in my life got to feel when I behaved a certain way, when I did something specific. So, you feel overwhelming joy, sorrow, and regret, but by seeing it from someone else's perspective, that's how you know who you are! You experience it from an outside source.

Me: Wow, that's interesting. Very interesting. And then what happened?

Erik: I realized how awful I was.

Me: Oh, no! You weren't awful, baby!

Erik: C'mon, Mom. I know you're my mom, but I was pretty difficult.

Me: No, I disagree. You got angry sometimes, like anyone does, but 99 percent of the time, you were very kind and sweet. Oh, my gosh, Erik. I mean, obviously you were troubled and had those moments of anger, but most of the time, you were so wonderful to others. I looked at all of your Facebook messages the other day, and so many of your friends were so shocked to hear of your death. They never knew you hid any darkness inside. [Your friend] Monica was so upset. She said you were always so happy and sweet; you always said hello and always stopped to talk, and most people did not know you were sad and angry inside. That was the disease talking, not the real Erik. Plus, I read your messages to some of your friends who were in pain. You told them you wanted to be there for them, to be a kind ear for them. Who does that as a teenager? You were very giving and special. I mean, you are.

[Long pause]

Erik: Wow! Hmm. I'm surprised, 'cause I felt like I was an open book.

Me: Maybe people just didn't bother really seeing.

Erik: But during the life review, you see it; you experience it and you feel it, and you judge yourself. No one is there to judge you but you. You think there's this guy on a golden throne with a staff pointed at your heart, you know, telling you to do twenty push-ups.

Me (laughing): I SMITE YOU!

Erik (laughing): Yes! But that's not it. When [your life is] over, you're left with yourself. You're left to think for yourself. I don't know whether I sat with my head in my hands for days or hours. All I know is that's the only place I was. And when it was all over, when I was done understanding who I was and what I did, then I could go back and—well, I didn't really go back. It's just like this silvery gray fog went away, and I found myself in a different place. I didn't feel like I was in control or like I was asking for certain things. I was just witnessing a process. I was just part of a process.

Me: What was that other place you found yourself in?

Erik: That's when [the gray fog] turned into gardens and paths, and my family was there. That's when it became social, like, "Let me show you around."

Me: Oh, yeah!

Erik: And they're like, "Let me show you what you're capable of doing. Let me help you."

Me: Who helped you the most? Was it somebody we know, or was it a guide, or—

Erik: There were a few, and it's hard to say who helped me most.

Jamie: He's talking about an aunt.

Me: Yeah, that'd be my younger sister Denise.

Jamie: A grandmother.

Me: Bestemor, Rune's mom.

Jamie: And a man who's not related to him.

Me: Okay. [Long pause.]

Jamie: Tell me about that man, Erik. [Pause as she listens to Erik.]

Jamie: The man. I keep hearing a name like Simon. It sounds so simple.

Erik: That's when I was able to make new friends—when I was able to understand the dynamics of the place where I was.

Me: And all during that, you felt very comfortable I guess?

Erik: Yeah, Mom. It was weird. If that had happened to me on Earth, I would have felt like I was being kidnapped.

Me: Oh, my God, yeah!

Erik: I would have been freaked out. But it was like, I felt warm all over. I couldn't cry. I couldn't cry if I wanted to. There was so much joy— silent joy—all around me. And when you feel that, you definitely don't wanna go jump back into your body!

Me: Do you have spirit guides over there? Do you have your own personal guides, like guardian angels that take care of you over there too?

Erik: Sure, but they're more like teachers.

Me: Oh, okay.

Erik: They do want you to learn for yourself, take care of yourself. We're not seen as helpless like we are on Earth.

Me: Can you actively participate in your life review by changing things since there is no linear time? It seems like you should be able to pre- empt the mistakes you made, you know?

Erik: Hell, that sort of defeats the whole purpose of the review, though, Mom.

[Jamie giggles.]

Me: Oh! So, that would be like changing the answers after you turned in the test, I guess?

Erik (laughing): Yes, exactly!

Jamie (chuckling): He made that drum sound—*duh dum dum*—like you get when you get the right answer.

Erik: No, you can't actively change it while you're reviewing it, but afterward, yes, since there's no linear time, you can. If there are things that you feel need to be corrected, and it serves the greater good or a higher purpose, then you're allowed to. But if it's negative and doesn't serve a greater purpose, you have to let sleeping dogs lie. That shit has to work itself out.

Me: I see. Exactly. Now, can your multiple selves in all of their simultaneous lives download or upload the information you learn in that life review, so that those other selves can apply it to their parallel lives? Oh, God, it's so complex. I can barely straighten out this thought in my feeble little mind!

Erik (laughing): No, I get it, Mom. You explained it fine. And yeah, sure, but those other lives on Earth have to have that knowledge of how to download that information. (a) They have to be aware of it—of the fact that they can do it; (b) they have to consciously want it; and (c) they have to be enlightened enough to understand how to use that information.

Me: So, it can't be done on a soul level, below the conscious ego level? Can you just go in like a stealth bomber and slip that information in nice and quietly? Call it a soul sortie?

Erik: Oh, there's so much more that happens at a soul level, but that soul level isn't what really runs your human life.

Jamie: Well, yes it does, Erik!

Me: Oh no! I'm on a runaway train with no conductor at the helm! This is not good!

Erik: Okay, let's put it this way: it's a happy balance between consciousness, spiritual amnesia, and soul-level stuff. You need that amnesia so that you can have new experiences. Without that, you're just a rat on a wheel.

Me: Okay, here's another one related to the whole life-review topic. If you kill scores of people, like in a war, do you feel each one's emotions during the review?

Erik: Hell, yeah. Their thoughts—like what they're thinking—what's happening, their emotions, what they feel—yes.

Me: Oh, my God. That must be brutal.

Erik: Definitely brutal.

It seems, from Erik's account, that the life review is one of the most valuable, teachable moments a spirit has after death and their transition into the afterlife. It makes sense of the struggles, the hardships, and the joyous memories that create the human experience—the reasons for our lives on the earthly plane.

7

THE ABILITIES OF AN UNTETHERED SOUL

Most of us cannot imagine "living" outside our bodies. In fact, most of us are under the impression that we *are* our bodies. Of course, most of our existence as eternal beings has been in the spiritual realm, unencumbered by that outer shell that so often brings us pleasure and pain, illness and health. So, what is it like to shed the physical body like a chrysalis sloughs its cocoon? What are the advantages? What are the disadvantages? Erik explains from his viewpoint as a newly untethered soul.

What Do Souls Look Like?

It's only natural for a mother to wonder if her child, in death, still looks the same as he or she did while alive. Erik's answers both surprised and comforted me.

Me: What do you look like, Erik? What shape do you take? Do you wear clothes? What age do you appear?

Erik: Hmm, well, when I'm hanging with my buds, I'm like a beam of light or a ball of light, but when I try to materialize there on the earthly plane, I appear the way I did before I died, so you guys know who I am.

Remember, Mom, I've had a lot of other lifetimes, and if I appeared as any one of them, you might not know it was me!

Me: Yeah, okay. That makes sense.

Erik: Now, when you get to the afterlife, Mom, I'll appear to you however you want. Do you want me to be a little boy? Do you want me to be grown up? You don't have to decide now. Wait till you get here, and I'll be whatever you want—or a beam or ball of light. You know, come to think of it, Mom, when you're in spirit too, it won't matter to you at all. It won't matter to you. You won't be going by how I looked when I was there. You'll just be interacting with my soul, which you will see and feel as a beam of light.

[At this point, I don't care what he looks like when I meet him again someday. I just want to wrap myself around him and love him. There'll be lots of pent-up kisses and hugs and love to deliver.]

Me: So, do your buddies appear to you as beams of light or as how they were when they were alive?

Erik: Balls of light, kinda like in that movie *Cocoon*, when they take their skin off. Oh, but we don't look like extraterrestrials or anything. We look like balls of light.

Me: Jamie, when you see Erik, what do you see? Do you see him, or do you just hear him, or what?

Jamie (laughing): I see him. Today, he has a T-shirt on. It looks kind of grayish in color, and it has some sort of print on it, but I don't see any words that go with it. Reminds me of an Ed Hardy design; you know, a pen-and-ink thing.

[I know exactly what shirt she's talking about. It has a very stylized, dragon-like image on it.]

Me: Oh, yeah, sure.

Jamie: It's short-sleeved, and he has jeans on.

Me: Of course. That's pretty much all he wore, even in our sweltering Houston summers.

Jamie: I can't really tell about his shoes; I think they're tennis shoes. They're not stark white, though.

Me (chuckling): Yeah, I bet not! Does he look see-through or solid to you?

Jamie: He's a bit transparent, not completely opaque.

What Can an Untethered Soul Do?

Once I opened my mind to the existence of life after death, I wondered what an untethered soul was capable of doing. Without an opposable thumb, I figured, the manual tasks you and I take for granted must be difficult. Again, Erik proved me wrong.

Erik: I'm helping my neighbor, this really cute girl, build a deck at her home.

Me: Oh, good!

Erik: Yeah, and I've got a motorcycle, a boat, a car. I like to work with the engines. I've taken up cooking too.

[My mind drifts back to fond memories of Erik concocting some amazingly creative dishes. His favorite was scrambled eggs in tandoori sauce, but a close second was eggs Benedict swimming in hollandaise. I remember how concerned I was that he'd develop heart disease at an early age from all the butter and cream he used. How silly those worries seem to me now.]

Me: So, you can work with your hands? It's not a matter of thought creating reality, like you think about the deck and it appears, and you think about a recipe and it's made? I mean, you can hammer in the nails and—

Erik: Yeah, I have the choice of either, but I like to work with my hands. Most people over here like to work with their energy instead of manifesting everything they want. We like to work with physical energy, 'cause then we feel a sense of achievement.

Me: You said you can morph into a bodily form. How do you do that, though, Erik? I just don't understand how you can manifest yourself in a physical form like that.

Erik: It's not about form. Go back to simple, eighth-grade science, Mom. Everything is energy.

Me: Uh-huh.

Erik: Our energy here moves at a quicker pace, so we can shape-shift, change [our] image, but faster. Also, you gotta remember, time is different here, so what you're watching might seem to take us one minute but actually seems longer in our perception. I might hang out with you for a minute in terms of your time, but it feels like hours to me.

Me: That's so fascinating, this whole time concept. I want to get into more detail with that, but first, I want to ask if you're able to visually materialize yet. I've seen you—uh, well, I don't know if I've really seen you or if it's my imagination, but I think I've seen you twice.

Erik (teasingly): Oh, Mom, you have. Of course you have!

Me: Okay! Is it really, really hard to do?

Erik: What, to materialize?

Me: Uh-huh.

Erik: Well, it does take a lot of focus, a lot of strength. I have to focus my energy down to match a wavelength and frequency you can see.

Me: Will you get better at it over time, so I can see you more?

Erik: Oh, yeah!

Me: Great! I so look forward to that. Now, I know you travel, Erik, but how do you do that? Do you use your thoughts? If you want to go to Norway, for instance, do you just think about it and you're there?

Erik: Well, it depends. I can materialize and dematerialize with my thoughts, like you just said, Mom, or if I want, I can take a boat or train or bus.

Me: So you manifest these things through thoughts?

Erik: Exactly. But I'm going to want to fly with you guys when you go to Norway for spring break. I don't have to stay on the plane the whole time, of course. I just do whatever I want to at the moment.

Me: Wow, lots of free choices there! Talk about traveling first class! And no standing in line at the security checkpoints. [changing subjects] Do you sleep, Erik?

Erik: No. I wasn't crazy about sleeping when I was there!

Me (in disbelief): Well, you sure did a lot of it!

Erik: Oh, I would do it when I had to or when I felt really depressed, to sort of escape things, but there were too many things to do when I was there. You remember how I used to like to stay up, Mom?

Me: Ah, yes, I do remember now. If you were excited about a new hobby or other interest, you'd stay up all night long.

Erik: Yeah. Then I'd sleep when I fell into an exhausted stupor. I always liked the idea of never having to sleep so I could stay busy, so now that I never have to, I love it! And you know what? Some spiritual beings here choose to sleep 'cause they like it, and they enjoy it, but I don't understand that. I think it's a waste of time. Not that time is the same here. It isn't.

Me: What do you do when you're not visiting us, like when we're asleep?

Erik: Oh! Well, I work on my bike; I go swimming with my friends; I go tubing; I go snowboarding. I've taken that up now, snowboarding. Oh, I do a lot of stuff. I either work on something mechanical, or I do something really active. I have a blast! I've made a bunch of new friends! They all passed from the earthly plane somewhere from the age of thirteen all the way to, like, twenty-eight, twenty-nine. Male and female. And we just have a blast. Sometimes it's hard to all get together, because we're all so active, but I'm trying to teach them about how important it is to keep in communication with the loved ones they left behind. You know what, Mom? Some of 'em never even thought about that! They never thought about it. They're like, "Well, you mean my parents and siblings would wanna keep talking to me?" and I'm like, "Well, fuck yeah!" So I'm encouraging them. You know where I got that idea, Mom? From you!

Me (beaming proudly): Aw, Erik, now you're helping people on both sides!

What Are the Differences between Incarnate and Discarnate Souls?

Me: So, Erik, what are the different abilities between free and untethered souls? What can you guys do on the spiritual plane that we can't do here? I know that your thoughts can create reality a lot faster, but what else is different about not having a body?

Erik: [There are three big] differences: Number one, we don't have any issues over here. Number two, we can manifest immediately whatever we want, like you just said. Number three, we all act at the highest level of our being. There is no awareness of hunger or thirst, being too cold or too hot.

Me: Gosh, why bother coming to Earth?

Erik: Well, it's cool [here], but it's sort of fun being there too, on Earth, because you make your own way, and it's sort of cool having no control over most things. That's why beings come back, not only to work on their levels of enlightenment and contribute to the lives of other people, but also because it's really exciting, in a perverse way, to let go of control and just be a part of something bigger than we are. And then you know what's so funny, Mom? We get there and all we do is bitch and moan and complain!

[I laugh in acknowledgment. He's preaching to the choir.]

Me: You know, that's so funny, because you completely surrender and you do so with a bang, when your soul goes into the body of an infant who's completely helpless! But are there some spirits who prefer the earthly plane to the spiritual one?

Erik: Yes, and vice versa. How many times have you heard a human go, "This is the last time I'm coming here" or "I'm not gonna do this again!" It kind of makes me laugh 'cause most of the time they'll be the first person to jump back into a body.

Me: Yeah, I guess if they're that disenchanted with their last life, they probably still need to come back!

Erik: Yep, and then there's the rare occasion when they're so connected to it, and they know this is their last time; this is what they have to do.

Me: You mean, sometimes they try to pack it all in to one last lifetime, so they make it a tough one?

Erik: Exactly.

Me: Okay, but if they want to come back just for grins and stuff, they can do it.

Erik: Shits and giggles? Yes.

Me (laughing): My God, Erik, that was just what I was going to say!

Erik: Yeah, I thought I'd correct you, Mom.

Me: Now, can you go into more detail about those three differences you spoke of, between free and untethered souls?

Erik: Well, as I've said, on the spiritual plane, you know, we can manifest anything we want in an instant. Everything is a thought away. We can travel anywhere we want—where I am now, throughout the universe, anywhere on Earth. We also have a complete memory and awareness of everything we've done in all of our past lifetimes: everywhere we've lived, everything we've said, everything we've thought, all the other souls we've interacted with. We have a memory of our level of enlightenment, what issues we still need to work on, when we might be going back to the earthly plane—uh, if we are.

Me: How nice to have that broader perspective!

Erik: Hell yeah. And over here, everyone is expected to have some sort of life's work, and this is mine. I mean, you can just be like a retired person and fish, plant a garden, paint, and lounge around in hammocks, so there isn't a "life's work police" that's gonna throw you in jail if you don't, but . . . We can live alone or in groups. Usually, we interact with the same group of souls over and over, and those are the ones who greet us when we come back here.

Me: I'm glad you'll be there to greet me.

Erik: Yeah, me too. On the earthly plane, we have spiritual amnesia about who we are, why we're there, what we're doing there, what our talents are. We forget we even have spiritual guides with us to help and direct us. And on the earthly plane, we forget how to manifest things like we do here in Heaven.

Me: Yeah, that sucks. It would make life so much easier if we remembered.

Erik: Yeah, but we often forget that we're there as humans to prevail over challenges rather than get derailed by them. We need to use challenges and traumas to fuel our forward movement, not stop it or drive it backward. Oh, and we forget why we're interacting with certain other souls. We don't put an emphasis on figuring out who we are and that we should have self-awareness. That kinda sucks, Mom, because that's what we need to do to see others for who they really are.

Me: Yeah, absolutely, Erik.

Erik: And if we don't have self-awareness there on the earthly plane, it's hard to figure out what our life's work is and then get into it. What happens is the ego sort of takes over that self-awareness or consciousness so much that, not only do we have no idea who we really are, we have no idea who other people are too. It's just ego-to-ego communication.

Me: Or ego-to-ego combat?

Erik: Yeah, that's right! So when we get to the earthly plane, it's kinda like one of those cartoons where, uh, like the Road Runner. Remember, Mom, the Road Runner? *Beep, beep!*

Me: Yeah, that's one of my favorites!

Erik: Yeah, and that coyote was always there trying to fuck him up—uh, I mean, give him grief. Like, a big anvil would fall off a cliff and hit the coyote instead of the Road Runner. Remember?

Me: Sure, Wile E. Coyote. I always felt so sorry for him! He looked so hungry.

Erik: Well, what I'm saying is that's how a lot of people feel when they get to the earthly plane, 'cause they don't have that self-awareness.

Me: Okay.

Erik: If you don't have self-awareness and direction, then you're gonna feel like shit, you're gonna feel depressed, and you're not gonna know what you have to look forward to. The ego sabotages itself at every turn. That's how it operates. [In a monotonous voice] Each day is gonna look like the day before.

Me: Exactly. That sort of describes how life was for you toward the end.

Erik: That's when you start asking yourself, *Why the fuck am I here?* A lot of people get stuck in that. It's really important to know what you have to look forward to; you can't really do that when you don't have self-awareness.

Me: Yep. I think we all go through periods like that. So, when we die, what additional information or secrets of the universe are we privy to? Any?

Erik: Anything we choose. Anything we want. Anything we seek.

Me: Wow! But I guess you have to be, you know, open to the possibility that the information is there, right?

Erik: That's true in the afterlife *and* on the earthly plane, Mom. The reason that Grandma doesn't "believe" is 'cause she's afraid. That's why I take her around places when she's asleep. We have a fuckin' blast visiting people and stuff.

Me (laughing): Wow, I hope you watch your language around her!

Erik: Are you kidding? She loves it, and she cusses like a sailor sometimes. Oh, one more thing, Mom. When we get to the earthly plane, we forget all about accountability.

Me: Oh, God, yeah.

Erik: We have certain things we're supposed to do, certain things we're supposed to say—

Me (chuckling): Some more than others too!

Erik (laughing): Yes. We forget what we're supposed to do and say on behalf of others who, uh, help show who we are and why we've even gone over there to the earthly plane. Holy shit, Mom, we go to a lot of trouble to go to the earthly plane!

Me: Yeah. Next time, I'm signing up for a trip to Disney World. More fun.

Erik: But that's why it's more difficult being born on the earthly plane than being reborn into the afterlife.

Me: Yeah.

Erik: Being reborn here, the soul pops out of the physical body. You have an immediate memory of who you are, and you let go of any physical discomfort. Lots of times when people die, they're in physical pain, and they get instant relief. It's intoxicating.

Me: Erik, you're being very poetic today! So, what do you miss most about the earthly plane? I know you can't speak for everybody, but in general terms—

Erik: Well, everyone is different, and what I miss has changed over time, Mom. Now: being able to physically interact with my family— you, Pappa, Kristina, Michelle, Lukas, Annika, everyone.

Me (sadly): Aww. I miss that too.

Erik: I also miss the anticipation of the unknown, because we don't have that over here. I kind of said that before.

Me: That excitement of not knowing everything—of relinquishing some control?

Erik (longingly): Yeah, and I miss how food feels in my mouth.

[Jamie giggles.]

Me: Anything else?

Erik: Yeah. The resistance when you go to touch something. The stop mechanism. That's part of why I miss the physical interaction with you guys.

Me: Oh, yeah. Okay. I guess it's hard to hug us here on the earthly plane when you just pass right through our bodies.

Erik: Yeah, 'cause we live in two different dimensions.

[Long pause as Erik thinks.]

Erik: Yeah, those are the main things I miss, I guess.

Me: I wish you could come and get those things all back again, but for you, I guess the pros outweigh the cons.

[Erik chuckles softly.]

Me: So, you travel through our bodies, Erik? Do you ever just fly right through since you don't have that "stop mechanism"?

Erik: Yeah, of course!

Me: What would that feel like to us?

Erik: It makes some people just take a deep breath.

[I can hear Jamie inhaling sharply.]

Erik: Like a gasp, like you can't get enough oxygen.

Me: Okay. I've had that happen a lot since you died! I just suddenly gasp for no reason.

Erik: Yeah, and some people will sneeze. So, it varies, but you definitely feel that gasp of, like, something just happened.

Me: Can you merge with a person?

Erik: Merge with a person?

Me: Yeah, with our consciousness. Can you merge with our consciousness when you're in there?

Erik: Yeah, for brief moments of time. But really, the human structure doesn't allow for it, at least not for more than a few moments at a time.

Me: So, from what you say, you're privy to all of that when you're on that side, then. So, do you see all your probable lives—present, past, and future?

Erik (laughing): "Privy"? Really, Mom?

Me: Hey, go easy on me. I'm just trying to say more than just my usual "okay," "uh-huh," and "yeah."

Erik: Yeah, I can tap into any of them, because they're all a part of "me."

Me: If a soul has been there before, shouldn't that soul remember how to live there? It seems like you describe some souls, including yourself, who had to relearn some skills.

Erik: For most people, there's a relearning period. The spiritual amnesia—

Me: Has to wear off.

Jamie (laughing): You guys are saying the same thing at the same time!

Me: Oh, my God, that's cool! So it's all about orientation, basically.

Erik: Well, think about it. Sometimes the body just dies so quickly and *SLAM!* You're right back in another place; your consciousness still wants to function as if it were a human being.

Me: Ah!

Erik: So there's gotta be some sort of wear-off, you know. And then you wake up and you realize your capabilities; they slowly come back to you.

Me: All right. That makes total sense. But when we die, do we become sort of all knowing?

Erik: Yeah, like a goddamn teenager.

Me (chuckling): Yeah, once they hit thirteen, they know it all!

[Erik laughs.]

Me: Okay, but do you gain knowledge about all the great mysteries of the world—heck, the universe? Do we know all the details of the world's history that are unknown today, great mysteries of civilization, like how they built the pyramids, who shot JFK, blah, blah, blah? In other words, do you become omniscient?

Erik: Those are all things you can find out, if that's your goal.

Me: Okay, so you can pretty much tap into anything. You don't automatically know these answers right when you cross over, but you can find them out. Is that what you're saying?

Erik: Yes.

Me: Okay, can you elaborate a little, Erik, so I have more than "yes" and "no" and short answers?

[Jamie laughs.]

Me: Unfortunately, we've gotten so good at communicating with one another that I tend to say what I think you're going to say before you get a chance to say it. Poor you—you can't get a word in edgewise!

[Erik laughs.]

Erik: When you arrive, what keeps you in a moment is your own focus. Right now, I'm focused on you. I'm here in this moment with you. I'm focused on you, but I can just simply change my focus to a different need and be somewhere else.

Me: Okay.

Erik: But in this moment, I don't need to know the makings or mysteries of the world. I don't need to know all these things. I could relax, broaden my focus, and receive that information. It's the same talent we have on Earth, though we refuse to use it. If you could open up your energetic body—that's the part that's really alive—everything here is a web of information to be tapped in to. As long as your belief system is such that you're open to even asking a specific question and you're open to its answer, you can access it. The physical body is fed by the energetic body. If we could open that up and allow more energy through, shit, we could do amazing things. Seriously, Mom, we could stop bullets; we could light fires; we could telepathically communicate; we could feed ourselves—

Me: That's awesome. Like the guy in *The Matrix*!

[Jamie laughs.]

Erik: Yes! We could speed up time; we could slow down time.

Me: Yeah, that's interesting, because I think time is created because consciousness moves through moment points. I guess that's a whole different story, though.

Erik: And so, if we can learn the techniques and adapt them to our everyday experiences, you'll find it has much more of a purpose and a use. But it's so sad, because we've been so stuck in the realm of point A to point B, our brains are taught to go through one, two, three, four, five—instead of doing what spirits do.

Me: Really? And what is that?

Erik: We just merge with information. We merge with all of it at once instead of gobbling it up piece by piece like a little Pac-Man.

Me: God, that'd be so much easier! I wish I could have merged with organic chemistry and calculus back in the day.

[Erik laughs.]

Me: Can you imagine? We could totally scrap the Department of Education or reconstruct it as the Department of Merging. Might even be able to get rid of all public schools! We could just tap in to all that information, just like they do in that movie *The Matrix*. You remember how Keanu Reeves would download all that information, like martial arts techniques and all that?

Erik: Yeah!

Me: That would be so awesome. Five minutes later, you're kicking some ass somewhere.

[Jamie laughs.]

Me: So, that's how spirits learn? They just tap into or merge with an energy field?

Erik: Yes! Yes! You merge right into it, and you bring it to the surface. That's how you can recall, and it's easy! But again, you have to be aware that the information exists. Like, if you don't even have any idea that kung fu exists, you won't know to tap into that energy. But if you are aware of martial arts, you might tap into information about kung fu. There's just so much! Mom, if you walked around with an awareness of every detail of every, every, every thing, where's your joy in simplicity?

Me: Oh, yeah! My last two brain cells are already in the throes of agonal breathing. If I downloaded everything, those two little guys would explode.

[Erik chuckles.]

[After Erik shared the amazing abilities that untethered souls have, I must admit that I felt pretty impotent. Since a single thought can't put a gourmet meal on the table this evening, I guess I'll have to slave in the kitchen instead. Since I can't think *Fiji Islands* and appear there in a nanosecond, I suppose I'll have to keep collecting those frequent flyer miles. Gotta work with what you have.]

Me: Let's talk more about how, as an untethered soul, you don't have the same emotional attachment to past-life issues as we humans do.

Erik (pointing at me): That's right, but you gotta remember that we don't lose our character. We kind of combine it with the base self. You know, 'cause we're looking at losing our incarnation, right? And if we have multiple incarnations at once, which is what we consider past lives, then multiple incarnations could be dying and coming back to base self.

Me: Yeah. Well, so does each self have a different personality? Let's take the whole multidimensional self; does it have a uniqueness about it as a whole? Like, does your multidimensional self have an Erikness; or is there one part of your multidimensional self that has an Erikness quality and another part that has another personality, like your evil twin?

[Jamie laughs.]

Erik (chuckling): No, it all stems from the same thing. It's all the same spiritual DNA; it's all the same package. The life that each part of the multidimensional self lives and chooses to live can shape them to have different angers or loves or hobbies. The core of it is exactly the same.

Me: I see. So the core is Erik, with the Erikness essence or quality.

Erik: Yeah, I'm all Erik.

Me: Okay. Anything else different about being untethered?

Jamie (chuckling): He pauses; he kind of looks up and goes, "It's just so much more free!"

Me: Yeah. Must be nice.

Erik: Fuck, yeah! And the other thing I wanna say about being here is you can never be right and you can never be wrong. You can only just be.

Me: Wow, that's good. Very different from the earthly plane, because here, there is always contrast; always duality; always right and wrong, winner and loser. You know what I mean, right?

Erik: Exactly, but that's why it's such a great classroom. One side has to understand the other. If a portrait has no contrast—I mean zero—it's just going to look all monochrome and shit. You're not gonna know who the hell it is in the picture.

Senses and Emotions

In discovering the different abilities of an untethered soul, I found myself wondering whether Erik could still taste and touch and smell, and in what way his emotions differed, other than having less emotional attachment to the past. As usual, Erik came through with some unexpected answers.

Me: Obviously, you can see and hear, Erik, but do you have your other senses? Can you taste and smell and touch?

Erik: If I choose to, sure.

Me: Do you feel cold and hot?

Erik: Only if we choose to. Like, I'm going to Norway with you guys during spring break, and I'll love feeling the brisk temperatures. I don't have to. I could be snowboarding and feel no temperature at all.

Me: What about other aspects of touch?

Erik: It's strange that we don't have that stop reflex I was talking about earlier. It's like when you put your hands to the wall, your fingertips stop when they touch the drywall. We don't do that. Our bodies move through the drywall; we *feel* the drywall. We feel the density of it; we feel the change of space. It took me a while to get used to that.

Me: Uh-huh.

Erik: So, holding hands with your girlfriend is very different over here. We can do it, but it's more like our hands are sharing the same space, merged together.

Me: Very interesting stuff, Erik. What about the other senses, like taste and smell? Can you taste the food you create and eat?

Erik: Ah, to a heightened degree, yes!

Me: Oh, really? Wow, but you don't have taste buds, so do you just go by the memory of those flavors?

Erik: Not only memories, but our energy can merge with what we've created, like food. That, in itself, heightens our senses. Our senses absorb that energy and give it a richer experience. So we can create it; we can look at it; we can define the colors, shapes, and sizes. We do have a sense of touch with food in our mouths, but it's more like a merging experience: with that comes texture; with that comes the emotions from the item, and with that comes the sense of taste. But it's more like it starts in the belly and goes outward, instead of staying just in the mouth. For taste, there's not just one place that gets it. That's how it is when we're humans: the tongue gets it.

[In another session, Erik explains how the human sense of physical touch—food against tongue—differs from the energetic creation of food and that energy merging with a spirit's energetic tongue.]

Me: Uh-huh.

Erik: Over here, the whole soul gets the experience. We have sound, of course. And then, there is smell, but it's kinda what I imagine a dog's sense of smell would be like. It's really heightened.

Me: Oh, okay. So, how do you bring forth smells to us? I mean, how does that happen? How do you work or manipulate energy to do all that?

Erik: You mean like when I make rotten fish smells or rank sock smells?

Jamie (laughing): Erik!

Me (chuckling): Uh-huh.

Erik: Well, everything has an energy formula on Earth, so I just replicate that energy formula, and I put it in that space. It's like a form of creation. Even though I know the material item behind the smell doesn't exist, I create the energy formula for its smell.

Me: Oh! Wow, how interesting! Okay, what about emotions? How do emotions change—like sadness, depression, and grief—once you are untethered?

Erik: Where I am, that just doesn't exist in the same way.

Me: But I remember you expressed that you felt deep remorse when you saw us grieve over your body. How is that different from the remorse people feel here?

Erik: Well, you know how people suffer from depression on the earthly plane: they feel like there's no way out, no doors, no windows, no light?

Me: Uh-huh.

Erik: If someone has depression here, all the doors would be open, all the windows would be open, and all the lights would be on. So, it's more difficult to stay in the moment of depression, but you can, if you're extremely focused on it. Others can see how you feel; you can't hide things here, Mom. And if I see someone focusing on depression, I have the choice of letting them have their moment, or I could send them more light. We all work in the way of community.

Me: Okay.

Erik: It's like we're not so attached to the lower emotions here. It's more objective and detached. It doesn't consume us like it does people on the earthly plane. Over there, you feel like you have to have the positive with the negative, the right with the wrong. Here, we just have what "is." All that is, *is*. It's a very harmonious existence. On Earth, we would define that as joyful or blissful.

Me: Okay.

Erik: So, you can have those focused pockets of jealousy, regret, sadness, and anger, but they're short-lived, and they feel very watered down.

Me: Can you hate over there in the afterlife?

Erik: If you want to, you can.

Me: Yeah, but do they, as a general rule? Does anybody hate?

Erik: Not really, no. It's very difficult to hold a grudge; to feel anger, disappointment, jealously. You can do it, but it's very difficult to hold on to.

Me: How come?

Erik: It just kind of goes against the natural flow. You have to exert so much energy to have it that you just normally give up, and you just end up seeing the—

Jamie (laughing at Erik): What are you rolling your eyes for? Seeing the what?

Erik: Seeing the better part of the emotion.

Me: So, it's like gripping on to monkey bars that are slathered with grease?

Erik: Yeah. Yes, yes, yes!

Me: Okay.

Erik: But I don't want people to think that there's a negative and a positive way to think about something. It's just that the denser energy is so much harder to hold on to up here that it's just not worth it. That's why people say that they feel such unconditional love when they have those near-death experiences and their whole life flips over. It's just because all that heavier shit on Earth doesn't translate.

Me: What do you mean, "doesn't translate"?

Erik: It's just, there's no room for it. Like I said, it's so hard to keep it here that you just don't want to anymore.

Me: So, it's just pushed away? Is that it? The denser energy is pushed away?

Erik: Yes.

Me: It's like oil and water, so—

Jamie (sounding surprised): That's the exact same thing he just said! He used the same metaphor!

Me: Very cool!

Dream Visits

What happens when our consciousness enters different states—when we sleep, when we dream, when we are in a coma or under general anesthesia? How do our deceased loved ones interact with us while we're in those various states? Erik shares what he knows about this fascinating subject.

Me: Erik, how exactly do you visit us in dreams?

Erik: Through electrical energy. You know how we can communicate telepathically, where my thoughts or words can pop into your head? It's one step beyond that. We use our electrical energy to manifest physically in a dream state, and then there's a step beyond that where we can manifest physically while you're awake. It's a whole lot easier when you're sleeping, though.

Me: Well, give me specifics. Do you clench your fists and grunt, or what?

[Erik laughs.]

Erik: I conjure up a feeling of goose bumps, so that it's strong; the more I practice, the stronger it gets, and it gets so strong that I can't stand it anymore, and it's like *pop!* I'm there in your dream. It's like I'm inside your head, but I'm also outside of you. It took me a little while to figure out how I can be inside your head and also outside of you at the same time, but now it's really easy.

Me: So, Erik, can I visit you, say, while I'm awake or about to go to sleep? Can I say, "My soul is going to leave my body tonight, and I'm going to the afterlife to visit Erik?"

Erik: Yeah.

Me: How can I do that?

Erik: Just talk to your soul, and tell your soul that's what you want to do.

[I can almost hear him say, "Duh!" I find this remark interesting, because I have recently begun to practice extending my consciousness to him.]

Me: Lately, I've been practicing visualizing your face and wrapping my arms around you—my soul around yours—and I feel something, an electrical connection.

Erik: I really feel that tangibly. Mom, you can really do that! *You're* doing that!

Me: What can I do to visit you at night when I sleep? How can I be sure that I'm going to have an out-of-body experience where I can come visit you in Heaven, or where we can work together, play together, spend time together—where we're soul to soul on the same plane? How can I do that?

Erik: I dunno. Ask your guides.

Jamie: Okay, guides, how can Elisa do that? [pause] Oh, I see. I see. They say you only have so much energy as a human being, and you're using a lot of that energy during the day to communicate, translate, and write. So you're not only using energy when you talk to Erik and your guides, but also with your writing as well, whether it's a blog, whether it's a screenplay, whether it's a book—no matter what it is. So the key for you is to build as much electrical energy as you can, and you will do that by communicating, [and] practicing your translating during waking hours.

Me (with a tone of doubt): Okay, that's good. I'll do that.

[I have a hard time practicing spirit communication and translation for the same reason I harbor a tiny smidgeon of doubt toward Erik's materializations and other visits—my pesky analytical mind. I know it entails a great deal of energy on my part, because I feel drained after trying to communicate with Erik for just a couple of minutes. Plus, my mind wanders to silly things like, "Did I unplug the coffee pot?" or "It sucks for Pluto that it's no longer a planet." Nevertheless, with clear marching orders in hand, I renew my commitment to work on these fledgling abilities. I'd do anything to be with my son in any way, shape, or form. After all, the umbilical cord never severs. If may get stretched pretty thin, but the connection survives even death. In another session, we continue our exploration into altered states.]

Me: Erik, are you aware of people who are asleep coming over to visit in the afterlife? In other words, when people are sleeping in bed, can they travel to the afterlife so that their physical bodies are in suspended animation, or some sort of "rest period" during which their guides watch over them?

Erik: Yeah, there is that, but it's not like some "sleeping hospital." It's not like the soul body floats themselves into Heaven and they line up in little rows. It's like—

Jamie: How do you explain what you're showing me, Erik?

[Long pause]

Erik: There are certain types of sleep where the soul is out of the body, like an out-of-body experience—

Me: Uh-huh.

Erik: During that moment, the soul could be "conscious awake" or "conscious asleep." When it's conscious asleep, it's as if the soul floats right above the body.

[Pause]

Erik: But it has that moment of outward experience, which is very freeing. It's a wonderful, healing experience to have a break from being in the body. The only resting period I know of, Mom, is when human beings choose not to move forward, or when guardian angels set up a resting period for a person if they need time to weigh, think, analyze, or just heal and recover before they move forward.

Me: Does only a part of the soul leave the body?

Jamie: The image he's showing me is almost like a double. Like, if you were sleeping on your back, there would be a double of you sleeping just a few inches above it—like double vision in a way. And what's interesting is that he's showing me that, as the person moves on the bed, the soul body moves above it. So it's still mimicking how the body's reacting, but it's a sense of freedom.

Me: Under what circumstances do people project part or all of their consciousness into the afterlife—do they ever do that? Or do they ever project their consciousness into other dimensions of any sort?

Erik: Let me finish, Mom.

Me: Oops, okay. My bad.

[Jamie and Erik both laugh.]

Erik: When they're asleep like that, what we can do is upload information to them. We can get up next to them; we can heal their energetic body; we can put more information in it, like upload stuff; we can alter a lot of shit in a positive way, but we can't screw around in a negative way.

Me: Okay, that's comforting.

Erik: Yeah, it's just not possible. That couldn't happen if the being had negative intent. No one can fuck you up like that while you're asleep. Call it a safety mechanism. But if that soul was "conscious awake" and out of the body, then that body can project into the afterlife—or whatever you wanna call it—across space and time. Hell, there can be full-on conversational lessons, you know, like teachings. I've done a little bit of that, but not a lot.

[Long pause]

Jamie (laughing): He—you still find that funny, Erik? He still finds it funny when people come out of or wake up physically in their bodies, like coming out of an out-of-body experience, where they kinda jerk into [their body].

Me: Yeah, I've heard some call it a crash landing.

Jamie: Yeah, he still thinks that's funny.

Me: Well, can a human being—the consciousness—leave and help others, you know, the other way around from what you've said?

Erik: Yes! Humans can willingly kinda sit back or lie down and leave their bodies. I have seen—

Jamie: Erik, use different terms so I know what you mean, like, just to clarify "alive" or "dead."

[Pause as she listens to Erik]

Jamie (insistently): Use "alive" or "dead"!

[Long pause]

Jamie: Oh, okay. So, he's saying he has seen a living person leave his or her body and help somebody who has just died—a "dead soul." And the "alive soul" is escorting the "dead soul" to the afterlife, to home.

Erik: There are "alive" people on Earth who do the work of escorting.

Me: How fascinating. Do they have any other roles in that regard? Do they ever just go visit another, uh, like a deceased relative or anything? I mean, well, of course I know they do that in lucid dreams.

Erik: They can, but a living person can completely be invoked without "knowing." They could be—You had this, Mom. *You* had this! You're completely awake and doing some routine thing like washing the dishes and all of a sudden you feel really, really tired.

Me: Sure.

Erik: And you're just so tired, you have to lie down. It's like there's no two ways about it; you're gonna go to sleep. You just don't know whether you're gonna sleep on the floor, the couch, or the bed. So you go for it, and you lie down. Those intense moments of needing to sleep—we call it "sleep," because that's how it feels to us; that's what our parents have said, like, "Oh, we have this feeling, and it's called 'sleepy,'" but that's not always the case. Sometimes it's just feeling the need to leave the body so you can go escort or help someone else. I mean, it could be 'cause it's the connection of a soul friend, a soul family, or somebody you promised—or you had made an agreement with—that you would be there to help them cross over.

Me: As one [blog] reader says, "This actually puts a totally different spin on which is the true reality—here or the afterlife. Do we wake up our soul to be in the afterlife, or do we wake up our bodies to be in the physical life? Maybe death is our soul waking up from a bad dream."

Erik (laughing): Bingo!

Erik: And what's cool is that you can't tell the difference between someone who comes to the afterlife during an out-of-body experience and a soul that lives in Heaven. We're all the same; we all have the same characteristics when the soul is out of the body. It's only when the soul goes into a physical body that it takes on different characteristics—physical, of course, but nonphysical too.

Me: Why are we sometimes more aware of our dreams—like, we're totally asleep, wandering around in the afterlife or whatever—and we don't remember what we've done when we wake up?

Erik: Some dreams are meant to help you record activities and thoughts that you've done or had in the soul's memory bank. Just recording, like you're hitting the "save" button. Then you might revisit places you've been and some of the things you've done as a way of, you know, replaying what the soul recorded. Also, there is some type of awareness, which the soul will direct you toward, that you don't need to remember when you wake up. Of course, other times you remember things with total recall. It's a perfect design. Your higher self knows exactly what needs to be sorted into the subconscious—like, on a soul level—and what needs to go to the conscious level to best help growth and progress. So, the things the soul wants you to remember on a conscious level, you remember.

Me: I see. That makes total sense.

Erik: If it's just recording what you've already done or said, and you've pretty much healed from it, or if it's something nonessential, you're probably not going to have recall.

Me: Okay. What about people who are in a coma—a vegetative state—or those who have brain damage? Tell me what you know about that.

Erik: Some of it is bullshit.

Me: Oh!

Jamie: I'm asking him why. What do you mean, Erik?

Erik: Even though the body doesn't function, like the eyes don't open, the fingers don't move, the body looks completely dead—it's just that we don't have the equipment to measure what the brain is actually doing. The ears are working and the person is having a conversation within, like an internal dialogue; but they can't get their mouths to open or their fingers to wiggle or their eyes to open to show you that they understand. As soon as [researchers] continue deeper studies into the coma state, they'll find that the brain will trigger certain patterns to show or give proof that the person inside is listening, comprehending, and is able to respond with an answer or a question.

Me: Okay. What about general anesthesia? Why don't we get out of our body and have an awareness, on a soul level, of our whereabouts?

Erik: Well, some people do!

Me: Oh, okay!

Erik: Some people do but not everybody, and that's gonna be based on beliefs. People have structures. Beliefs exist—

Me: Okay, so you're saying it's basically about belief. Some people don't believe they can maintain an awareness during general anesthesia because they don't think of their soul as a separate, aware entity—

Erik: Right.

Me: Okay, so they just hang on to their body, wired to their shut-down brain?

Erik: Yep.

Me: So what's the difference between sleep and the out-of-body experience where you're aware of your situation and surroundings?

Erik: Well, with sleep, the soul is still connected to the physical body. With the out-of-body experience, the soul is no longer residing inside the physical body. It's outside the frame of the physical body.

Energy Work

Everything—even objects that seem solid to us in our limited three-dimensional perspective—is energy. In fact, Albert Einstein referred to matter as "frozen light." So, imagine having the power to manipulate and control that energy! We do have such power, in a limited way, here on the earthly plane, but Erik and his afterlife cohorts have a near-infinite ability to do so, especially with practice.

Me: How is the practice going, working with your energy, Erik? What are you able to do now? Also, how do you practice? Does somebody teach you?

Erik (with a short chuckle): Well, there are classes, but you know me: I just like to try something on my own! It's going really well, Mom! I've been materializing at home as balls and beams of light. I've been moving material objects. I've been sitting next to you while you drive, copiloting and talking to you. I think it's going really well. The dog sees me really clearly and so does the baby, Arley [Erik's niece]. She and I are getting along well.

[It doesn't surprise me that he's been skipping his "energy manipula-tion" classes. He never was enamored with the classroom setting.]

Me: How do you practice, exactly?

Erik: By doing it, just like you practice your communicating and trans-lating by doing it—just like you have to practice things on the earthly plane by doing it.

[I'm still puzzled. I have no idea how we mere humans work with our energy, short of plugging in the toaster or filling the car up with gas. So I push harder yet.]

Me: I can't imagine how you practice manipulating energy, but I guess, once you're on the other side, it becomes more obvious?

Erik (in mock exasperation): Well, Mommmm! *You* always do it. How do you think you heal people?

[Um, okay, this doesn't exactly clarify things.]

Me: I don't know. Good question.

[Surely he could detect the hint of sarcasm in my voice.]

Erik: You take your electrical energy, and you put it into other people's bodies. You manipulate energy all the time!

[Arrgghhh! I just want step-by-step instructions, like, "You put your right foot in, you put your right foot out, you put your right foot in, and you shake it all about," but clearly it's not going to be that simple.]

Me (impatiently): By imagining it? By thinking about it? How?

Erik: By visualizing. When you visualize energy [(a healing treatment)] projecting into a material form, it happens.

[Okay, that answer satisfies me for the moment, so I go on to another question.]

Me: Did you visit us in Norway by manipulating your energy into a physical form?

Erik: Sure, I was there the whole time, Mom. Don't you remember seeing me in your bedroom?

Me: Well, yes! I felt like I was fully awake, but the skeptic in me wonders if I was in a dream state or imagining things. Damn my analytical mind.

Erik: Mom, it's going to take you another three and a half months before you absolutely, positively, without question, feel totally confident that I'm there and know how and when I communicate with you. There's going to be another trip to Norway before the end of the year, and you're going to pick up on me really strongly there, but you'll pick up on me really strongly everywhere by then. I'm going to be such a tangible presence that you'll be talking out loud to me, and people will be looking, saying, "Hmm, so who is this woman, who seems to be alone, talking to?" Also, other people will see me too. They'll be like, "Oh, there are three of you to be seated?" when there's only you and Michelle. I'll be more and more tangible.

Me (with hopeful enthusiasm): Good! I'm so proud of you, Erik! How can you move things? How do you move objects on the earthly plane? For example, you've made coins, confetti, and Airsoft pellets appear. Do you just create it or do you move it from its original location?

Erik: If we're bringing in something new, we create it; but if we were to move a glass on the table, then we would create a denser energy behind it to push it along. It's like you using the denser boundaries of your skin, your hand, to be able to push against the glass and move it.

Me: That is so very cool, Erik, and it makes complete sense! So, how do you move yourself from one area to another?

Erik: By projecting my consciousness. I just visualize my electrical energy being here or being there, and *boom!* I'm where I visualized myself. Mom, it's just like if you visualized being in Venice, Italy, and you were able to transport yourself there in the next instant.

Me: "Beam me up, Scotty!"

Erik: I'm still learning a lot. I can come easily to you and a few others, but if I was to go out and assist somebody I didn't know very well, who was having some issues, that would be harder. I'm learning how to do that now so I can guide people. The ones that need the most guidance are the hardest to get through to. So it's all about focusing your intent, your energy. It's really easy to focus on you and everyone I love, but those who I don't know—that takes extra training.

Me: Why is that, sweetie?

Erik: It's learning to move around—we can go anywhere we want, you know. But it takes a lot of training, kinda like a pilot has to train. It takes focus and a certain type of ability. I can see everywhere, but to actually go and move about, that takes time to learn.

Me: So, going to the "stranger in distress," so to speak, homing in on them, is more difficult than going to places you know, like our house or the houses of blog members you know?

Erik: Yeah, it takes energy. We have a lot of energy, but still, it's learning how to control it.

Me: Yeah, I bet. Do you ever get worn out?

Erik: I get tired, sure, but a different kind of tired. Yes, your energy can drop a little, but not like it was on Earth for me. That was different.

Me: Why can I move things like a can of Coke, but you say it takes so much energy for you to do it? I thought untethered souls had more energy than incarnate ones.

Erik: Okay, Mom, okay. I'll tell you what, Mom, sit down at the table with that can of Coke, whether it's empty or full, then *you* try to move it without touching it! See how easy that is!

Me: Yeah, I see your point!

Erik: You see, the can is in the physical plane, and so are you. As spirits, we have to move everything with energy, period. If you have arms, hands—

Me: Yeah, we have matter (our hands), which we can use to push matter.

Erik: Yeah, we're talking apples and apples. If you sit down and try to move the can with your energy, see how simple that is! You could! You could get to that point.

Me: Wow, really?

Erik: Yeah. And once you can do that, Mom, then we'll talk!

[We all laugh.]

Me: I'll get right on it, sir! But I've seen you move plates full of food, pepper shakers, and other things pretty long distances, so you must be growing by leaps and bounds in that regard!

Erik: Yeah. I'm getting the hang of it.

Life's Work

Just as I poise myself on the precipice of retirement, I discover that there is work after death. Never can catch a break, can we? But apparently, untethered souls adore what they call their "life's work." To delve into this further, I ask Erik a few broad questions, with the help of Kim O'Neill:

Me: Do souls have some sort of specialty in the afterlife, like a life's work?

Erik: Sure, all of us have different gifts and talents.

Me: So, what's your life's work over there?

Erik: Right now? It's bringing to light the story of teen suicide. My life's work now is teaching and healing, just like yours is. It's about helping anyone, especially kids and teens. I feel totally excited and focused on this; I feel fulfilled! Mom, Mom, Mom! I feel like a have a sense of calm and peacefulness!

Kim: Erik, are you tired?

Erik: Yeah, kinda.

Kim: How can you be tired in spirit? I'm just asking.

Erik: Well, I had a big night last night.

Kim: But in spirit, without a physical body to recharge—

Erik (in mock frustration): Can we just get on with it?

Kim (chuckling): Okay, okay! Let's see what he wants to tell you.

[Pause]

Kim: Oh, he's giving me a hug!

Me: Aw!

Kim (tearfully): He's giving me a hug! Aw! He says he was working; that's why he's tired! He says that now, because of your blog, a lot of people from all over the world want to talk to him, and so he's been trying to figure out how to do it.

Erik (laughing): It's like that movie, Mom. That Jim Carrey movie about God.

Me: *Bruce Almighty!*

Erik: Yeah, holy shit! There are a lot of people out there! So, I'm trying to figure out how I can talk to everybody. I dunno, maybe I'll put 'em on a schedule, Mom. I dunno. If I do it like Kim, I'll never get to everybody! You know, how she sets people up by appointment?

Me: Yeah.

Erik: And there are only so many people she can talk to in a day, and then her energy runs out. I'm trying to figure out how to do it.

Me: You need balance over there too! Is this all too much for you?

Erik: No, I'm not saying that, and I'm not asking you to help me, Mom. I'll figure it out. I don't want to give you more responsibility than you already have. You're pretty much maxed out. This is just something I'm going to have to figure out.

Me: What other kinds of work can you do on the "other side"? I know you have a job working with me to help people over here, so I'm sure there are others who do the same, but are there beings who rescue people who are confused after they cross—like skeptics, atheists, and people who have rigid religious beliefs? In other words, what are all the types of work that people do in the next phase of life?

Erik: A guide, like what I'm doing—that's like being a taxicab driver in New York City. It's very common over here. A lot of spiritual beings are just retired too. They don't really have a placement or position. They're here to see family, to experience joy, to travel to other places, stuff like that.

Me: Save that job for me. Sounds fun. Do they get retirement benefits?

Erik (chuckling): Thank God we don't have to have money over here to survive!

Me: Oh, I wish we didn't need it on the earthly plane. It just seems to create obstacles, divisions, and frustrations. Okay, so you can have a little home, sit in a living room, and eat pizza. Are there actually pizza-delivery people? Are there bookstore clerks? Other occupations?

Erik: Yes, there are historians. Now, the word "historian" on Earth means everything in the past, but a historian for us is a person who's so aware of time and time loops, they can talk past, present, and future. There are also spirits who help us reincarnate—who help us look at our life plans, you know, sorta like counselors. They help us consider each life plan to see what effect it'll have. There are [also] healers, like your doctors on Earth. When we die and our energy is torn, they help us mend and heal. Those doctors are also similar to teachers; they show us why this occurred, why the energy got messed up. Everybody works together.

Me: That's fascinating. So, are there beings who have typical "earthly plane" jobs, like bus drivers?

Erik: No. We don't have a system that really requires that. Like you asked about pizza deliveries? We can manifest our own pizza instantly, or we can manifest an oven and all the ingredients to make it ourselves. We don't need buses, 'cause we travel instantly by thought. But if we want to experience driving a bus or going around in a Domino's pizza-delivery car, we can.

Me: Yeah, I figured that'd be the way it is.

Erik: We have artisans. We have organized music. We do have all sorts of groups we participate in.

Me: Okay, but no carpenters or plumbers, or anything like that?

Erik: Nah, building isn't necessary because we create from the inside out. I could create a hammer and some nails and wood to build something if I wanted to, and I could just hammer away, but . . .

Me: Yeah, okay.

Erik: Oh, and to your question about rescuers, yes, we have people who guide the newly deceased, but usually these are ancestors, family members, and friends. If someone is hung up on some belief system and creates this nothingness to float around in 'cause they don't believe in an afterlife, eventually someone will rescue them and help orient them. Usually, they come around on their own, once they realize they're still able to have thoughts. Their vibrations slowly open up and get higher, and those thoughts create an afterlife for them. The same thing goes for people who believe they should be in Hell.

Me: So, it's good that no one is stuck in nothingness or fire and brimstone forever!

Erik: Aw, no! That could never happen!

Me: How did you choose this work, Erik? Were you ever a guru in the past, or are you just somebody who's learning to be a guide, learning as you go?

Erik: They knew, when I came, what my gifts were. And you know that I really did like to learn [on Earth], but I wanted to learn what I *liked* to learn, not what they were teaching me.

Me: Exactly!

Erik: So, for me, [the afterlife] is so fascinating. Life on Earth was very complicated, and there were so many inconsistencies—people saying one thing and doing another. That was one of my biggest issues.

Me (sadly): Yeah.

[I know he was referring to his friends who would seem loyal one minute and shun the next.]

Erik: So, I can help. From where I am now, I can help all those others who are just like me—confused. Mom, I never realized that there are so many others who really feel like I did—almost like they don't belong. I knew I belonged to you and the rest of the family, and I can't tell you how wonderful that was, but I felt like I didn't belong in the world.

Me: Me too. Sometimes I don't feel like I belong here on the earthly plane either. It feels alien to me sometimes.

Erik: Yeah, but Mom, look what you've done!

Me: Yeah, I like some parts of life here, of course, but I feel somewhat awkward. I feel much more comfortable in the spiritual realm, I think. I'm one of those!

Erik (with sympathy): Yeah, yeah. Yes, yes. That I can see.

Me: Yeah.

Erik: Back to your question about life's work [for souls] over here. We can choose to do whatever we want. We can choose to landscape; we can choose to be a guardian angel; we can help souls who are just arriving and who aren't happy about being here, uh—

Me: Well, since you can travel anywhere by thought, obviously there aren't any taxicab drivers, are there?

Erik: Like I said, we can choose anything we want. Say driving a cab was something we really enjoyed on the earthly plane. We might want to do that sort of service over here for people. Maybe some souls like riding around in cabs. We can choose to materialize here and there in the afterlife; we can manifest whatever we want, you know, in a moment. We can live in whatever environment we choose and do the work that we want, so of course we can conjure up a cab and drive around in it, and of course we can hail a cab and ride around in it. Plus, cab drivers here have better attitudes, and the ride is free!

Me (laughing): I hope the cabs smell better than some of the ones over here!

[Erik laughs.]

Me: What do they like to call that place where you live and work now?—"the afterlife," "the other side," what?

Erik (thinking for a moment, furrowing his brow and then shrugging): There are lots of names for it—and they're all good—but I prefer to call it "home." Sometimes I'll call it Heaven 'cause I know a lot of people will understand that name.

Soul Level

A soul is a soul is a soul, right? Not according to Erik. In the following session (with Kim translating), Erik explains the basic differentiation of soul hierarchy.

Me: Are there different levels of souls according to different levels of enlightenment? If so, are they different colors? I mean, how does the whole hierarchy thing work out?

Erik: Sometimes the light emitted by souls is different colors, but it has nothing to do with our enlightenment. It has to do with colors we like. With Kim, she would emit a blue light.

Kim: Yeah, you're right, Erik! Blue is my favorite color! You're right!

Me: So, are there different levels of enlightenment?

Erik: Different levels of enlightenment—yes, yes. They're not segregated, but you sort of hang out with the souls who are of the same caliber you are, or with souls you've been with before, for many past lifetimes—who have been either your students or your teachers. Oh, and kindred spirits too. I mean, everybody interacts with everybody else, but you kind of hang out with souls you've been with before. Everybody is [at] a different level of enlightenment, and [the level] depends on lots of things, like the age of your soul, but that doesn't necessarily mean anything. Somebody can be an asshole and be an old soul. So being an old soul means nothing. It's what you've done with your time, both on the earthly plane and here.

Me: So, if you're too lazy or lack the courage to work on issues while you're alive, then you might be an old soul, but you'd have a lower level of enlightenment?

Erik: Yep, you got it.

Me: Well, how do you know? How do you know how enlightened you are as a soul?

Erik: When your soul pops out of the body, it has a complete remembrance of everything, and then you review how you did in that lifetime. Did you do everything that you could have or should have? You judge yourself. Well, I don't want to use the word "judge"; you measure. You measure how well you did, and then you just try to do better. When you're here, there isn't a lot of emphasis on self-criticism. Here, we all realize what a waste of time that is. That's another really big difference between the afterlife and the earthly plane. You know how people are so self-critical, they criticize themselves so much on the earthly plane? Total waste of time! If they just focused that energy into improving themselves! Now, don't I sound like I know jack shit about everything? Ha! How long have I been here? Not long. But I've learned a lot, and, Mom, I'm still going to therapy.

Me: Good, sweetie. So, do you go from one level to the next as you—

Erik: Oh, yeah. It's not really levels— It's hard to explain. Mom, you know one of the hardest things for us here is to explain stuff to you who are still on the earthly plane, 'cause we have to translate it into a sequential language. And since things are not sequential here, sometimes the message gets a little garbled, but—

Me: Well, I'll try not to use the term "level," but what is your status in the afterlife, Erik? Are you a messenger of some sort? I mean, you seem to interact with humans so easily, and the impact you have on everyone is causing a huge ripple effect that's bound to have an impact on even more people. Some of the blog members feel like you're of a much higher vibration or maybe just a different vibration.

Erik: Well, I am a guide in training, and nothing I've ever done feels like this. Mom, you're filled with such light, and the more I learn, the wiser I become and the more light is inside me. We're all working to shift the collective consciousness toward spiritual enlightenment so that the Earth doesn't have to go through such a dramatic and traumatic change. I never thought that I'd be doing something this important!

Me: So exciting. I couldn't be more proud. So, Erik, do you have a personal guide where you are? If so, what name does he or she go by?

Erik: I have a lot of guides.

Me (laughing): Ah, you need all the help you can get, eh? You and me both!

Erik (chuckling): Well, me more than you now!

Me: I don't know about that!

[Erik laughs hard.]

Erik: I'm going to school to learn how to work better with you and how to connect with other beings—both of the light and of the Earth, in the spiritual realm and on the Earth. I'm going to be an instructor! I just know it!

[I laugh at his boyish charm and confidence.]

Erik: I'm going to be instructing others who are just coming over. So there are teachers, guides, angels. . . . I can give you names if you

want, but it's all energy. Everyone recognizes everyone else through
their energy.

Therapy

According to Erik, those souls who cross over after challenging lives,
those who have suffered traumatic deaths, and those who have committed suicide usually undergo a period of therapy. Some spirits are
specifically trained to heal the torn or shattered energy of these souls, as
well as to help them benefit from the hardships they endured, turning
these trials into valuable tools for spiritual growth.

Erik: Mom, I wouldn't have had calm and peace here if I hadn't had
therapy over here. People need to know that you don't magically feel
that peacefulness emotionally once you're back in the afterlife. Sometimes you feel a whole lot more pain than when you were on Earth.
That's what we need to make clear. It's not just, "Oh, I'm a spirit! Everything is happiness and light!" It's all about healing. You can run from
this shit, but you can't hide. You've gotta do the healing. And sometimes the healing is easier to do on Earth, but people don't realize that.
So, we're gonna help them learn that, Mom, aren't we?

Me: Good! I'm with you all the way! Erik, can you tell me a little more
about the therapy you went through when you crossed over? It's hard
to imagine spirits lying on a couch in a therapist's office, talking about
childhood bullies and strict parents. How does it all work?

Erik: I had individual therapy just like on the earthly plane, where I
would go sit and talk, but it's a little different in the afterlife, because the
therapist talks a lot more here. I'm really familiar with how therapists
talk on Earth, you know—how they try to get the patient to talk and
come up with realizations. Here, it's a combination, though—a give
and take. And it's private just like on the earthly plane. I lucked out
'cause my therapist is really hot.

[I chuckle, remembering his love of beautiful women.]

Erik: Yeah, and they also conduct group sessions, which are especially good for souls returning to spirit after having committed suicide or who had a violent death, like a murder or an accident, and also souls who had a very swift illness. These [deaths] are all kind of shocking to the soul, so they have to "regroup" in group. It's a shock to the emotions even if a soul had a destiny to die in that certain way. They still need therapy to help them get beyond it, but therapy here in the afterlife is usually really fast. Souls are really eager to heal and move on. That's very different from therapy on the earthly plane, 'cause here we want to heal much faster and are willing to heal much faster.

Me: What are the specific kinds of therapy that souls get? Can you tell me in general terms what sorts of things are talked about?

Erik: I don't know about therapy others have had. I can only tell you what sort of things I talked about. [My therapist] helped me see how some of my past lives affected my last lifetime, and Mom, it really felt good! It felt so good to let go of all of that. I've been thinking and thinking about it. I can't get over how many issues I was lugging around and how heavy it all was! It's amazing that human beings can even put one foot in front of the other and live their lives, lugging all that heavy baggage behind them. You don't know how much shit you're carrying around; you don't know how heavy it all is until you go through regressions on Earth, or until you get over here and get into therapy. It's just amazing how quickly you can let it all go—how you can acknowledge what you went through and then let it all go! I still can't get over it.

Me: Yeah, I'm so glad that you're happy and at peace now; that's all that counts.

Erik: Yeah, that's true.

After diving into these conversations about the soul and its possibilities in the afterlife, it became clear to me that Erik has gained his bearings in the afterlife. When we first communicated shortly after his death, he seemed confused and disoriented. But now I know that he has his footing, because of the many wonders he has shared, and by the confidence and comfort he displays as an untethered soul himself. He is no longer in his physical body, but he knows how to function in his current form and how to take advantage of this form's enormous abilities, particularly the ability to create his own reality—to make a life for himself in exactly the way he wants—which is something he was never able to do while he was alive on Earth.

Since Erik's death, I have taken time to compare the relationship we share now to the one I had with him before his death. In many ways, it is not very different, apart from the stark absence of physical affection, which I miss very much. When he was alive, I did everything I could to guide Erik toward a fulfilling life lived with a sense of purpose and relevance. All of my efforts seemed to be in vain, however, because Erik was never interested in his future; it was all about the moment for him. Perhaps, deep inside, he knew that his future lay elsewhere. Today, I still strive to guide and support him toward personal fulfillment, only now I do so by helping to be his voice here on Earth.

8

THE NATURE OF THE AFTERLIFE

As I mentioned earlier in the book, understanding the concepts and constructs of Erik's whereabouts as an untethered soul, and what the afterlife was actually like, was perhaps my most important goal in seeking out this new relationship with my son. How I wanted to make sure he was in a good place and in good hands! I found both relief and illumination in the following conversations with Erik about the nature of the afterlife. I hope this information brings as much comfort to you as it has to me. The most vital thing that I wish for you, the reader, to take away from our conversations in this section is that the afterlife is a place where the possibilities are endless and where we are truly at home when we leave our bodies. Erik has described the afterlife as a sea of unconditional love—perhaps the only place in which we are willing to drown.

What Does the Afterlife Look Like?

Me: Erik, what does the afterlife really look like?

Erik: Anything you want it to! Picture life on the earthly plane as living with a really, really gray pair of glasses on. Here, the colors are more vivid than you can ever imagine—a hundred times more than on the earthly plane. [The afterlife] looks like whatever appeals to you

135

at the moment. Where I am now, the grass is purple, and it's so beautiful. There are flowers everywhere, and you hear music all the time. They tell me that music is the link between the afterlife and Earth. It's vibrational. It's so cool, Mom—all the information that you get from here. And it makes so much fucking sense. You know, when I was there with you, things didn't make sense to me: the people and their problems, the wars, and all that disharmony—it just didn't make any sense. There were so many contradictions—people saying one thing and doing another. But here, it's so different. It's actually very beautiful. There are others here that I see, and there are even animals. Do you know that I can talk to animals here?

Me: Oh, boy, that's wonderful, baby!

Erik: Yeah, and I sure love that. I know, with your work, you've seen death. So I'm hoping that this helps you—you know, my explanation of what it's like here. I can just say it's the coolest thing! There are places here, like big coliseums, where you can go, and there's music! There's love everywhere, and you know the old saying that love heals everything? Of course I've heard that when I lived there, but I see now how true that really is.

Me: It sure does help me sweetie. Okay, so you say that, where you are now, the grass is purple. Is that only for you or everyone else too? In other words, can you and another soul be right next to each other and see a different landscape?

Erik: Well, we can do both, Mom. We can see the same landscape through the other person's "eyes," because, listen, listen—

[He's very excited at this point in the conversation.]

Jamie (chuckling): He's got his palms up toward the ceiling.

Erik: Listen, Mom, if the person's sitting next to me, they're sitting in my energy, and when we do that here, we can merge perspectives and merge our consciousness with the other one's consciousness. So, if I'm perceiving the purple, shiny grass, then the person sitting next to me can see through my eyes what I'm envisioning—and I can see through his.

Me: That is awesome, Erik! Now, what if you and your buddies want to go surfing at a beach. Do you have to create this reality as a collective?

Erik: Yeah, but there's so many people who have that same desire, so these beaches [already] exist, and we can go to that place any time.

Me: Oh, I see! Can one buddy snow ski while you surf, while still being in the same proximity?

Erik: Yep. You can have a created realm on top of another created realm. It's amazing, Mom.

Me: Plus, you don't have to break a leg or get eaten by sharks!

[Erik laughs.]

Day to Day in the Afterlife

Me: Now, Erik, why is it that the afterlife you describe looks almost like the earthly plane in some existences?

Erik: Yes, La-Z-Boys and pizza. Mom, that's what our lives on the earthly plane trained us for. These are our memories and our thoughts, still wanting to be alive. These are our comforts, still wanting to be alive.

Me: Ah! Okay.

Erik: And so we create them. We create these comforts with those memory thoughts. Not everybody does, though.

Me: Yeah, yeah.

Erik: But it's really wonderful.

Me: Yeah. And when you create such surroundings, that's where your vibration is—more at an earthly vibration?

Erik: Yeah, and it's great, because we're never going to run out of space!

Me (laughing): I guess not! So, how do you meet other beings in the afterlife? Does there have to be some sort of connection, like past lives?

Erik: No, there doesn't have to be a past connection, 'cause we're all connected anyway. But there are these soul families that reincarnate together. They can be anywhere from really, really big to very small, and you're greeted by your soul family when you cross over. Of course they've made friends and you've made friends. You can just think of somebody and they're there. Just like when you think of me, Mom. Then I'm there. Oh, or if it's somebody famous like Michael Jackson, you can just think of him and inquire to engage with him. It's kinda like using a telephone, but you don't really need a number.

[Jamie and I laugh.]

Erik: And we do have social events!

Me: Oh, cool!

Erik: We have music, like I said before, and we have—I guess you could call them dances, but they're different. We have gatherings, talks. It's kinda like how I'd imagine it would be to sit on the steps of the Parthenon, like all the Greek philosophers sitting around, talking about astrology. We have these talks, and we talk about the faith and the fate of the Earth, and we talk about how we can be involved and how we can help.

Me: That sounds amazing! All right. Do you have hospitals, schools, shopping malls, restaurants, or any of the other establishments that we have here on Earth?

Erik: Well, no restaurants, 'cause we don't need food. There's music, choirs, dancing—beautiful. There are gardens and animals, and libraries everywhere. There are books of such wisdom, you can't even imagine! You can learn about anything in the universe and about any being from other worlds—and there are other worlds, universes, and dimensions, Mom. There aren't any hospitals like you have them where you are, 'cause we don't really need medical care, but there are places for energy healing, like healing centers. This is especially for those souls who first cross over here like me or others who died of a sudden illness or had traumatic lives or deaths. It's more like a resting place with healers and angels. There aren't any movie theaters, because we can see all we need to see when we watch the Earth. We can see, you know. I visit you, and that's better than any movie.

Me: Aw! But can you and your friends create [things like this] if you wanted to?

Erik: Yes, if you want that experience. We have gatherings with friends and family—there's family here, of course. Lots of play. There are schools all over. All of us who come here learn some sort of craft or skill. Some learn how to be energetic healers, while some train to be guides like me.

Me: So, you say you have a flat-screen television over there; what kind of programming do you watch?

Erik (with a big mischievous smile): Whatever we damn well please!

[Erik laughs hysterically at his own retort.]

Erik: Mom, it's so great, because like I said before, we can watch whatever programs we want whenever we want.

Me: Celestial on-demand television!

Erik (laughing): Exactly. While I sit and eat my pizza.

[Erik, Jamie, and I laugh hard.]

Me: Do you guys in the afterlife celebrate holidays? Like, do you have Mother's Day, death anniversaries, birthdays, Christmas, Chanukah, and all that?

Erik: No, not really. We celebrate, though. A lot of times we celebrate— since we're so close to the Earth—the changing of the Earth's seasons, but we also celebrate the day we come in, which would be our birthday, really.

Me: Yeah, that makes sense.

Erik: But just remember, Hallmark made most of these holidays, Mom.

Me (laughing): I know!

Erik: We don't have Hallmark!

[Jamie laughs.]

Layers and Levels

As a human, I'm accustomed to my environment having structure, including various regions such as neighborhoods, shopping centers, schools, and downtown. I asked Erik to share whether the afterlife has a similar structure.

Me: So, [are there] regions of some sort [in the afterlife]? You know how here we have The Heights, Piney Point, River Oaks, The Fifth Ward, and so on?

Erik: All the energy is layered, Mom. On the earthly plane, there is no differentiation between layers of souls like there is over here.

Me: Okay. Is it layered by densities, like water and oil?

Erik: Like that, yeah. Not exactly, but—

Me: So, your ability to move from one layer to the next, Erik—is that based on your vibrational density?

Erik: Right. And as my vibrational density decreases with my spiritual evolution, I can enter the vibrational-frequency layer that matches mine. It allows my energy to move through other energies. At my current density, I can move through energy layers that are at the same or greater density, but only when my vibrations get higher I can move up to the lighter, less dense layers. It's not a hierarchy in the superior/inferior sense, though. It just is what it is.

Me: So, are you saying that parts of the afterlife differ in terms of vibrations or energy?

Erik: Different "areas" of the afterlife are based on different intensities and kinds of energy. I say "area" even though this is really not a two- or three-dimensional realm, but I have to use this to explain it in a way you'll understand. You can look at it in terms of vibrational levels. In certain vibrations, your perspective is narrow, and in others, it's broader.

Me: Okay. So, the lower vibration, is your [perspective] narrower?

Erik: Yes. Like we were talking about atheists; they don't [choose to] believe [in] anything. They have a narrower vibration; they have a different vibrational afterlife. But when they reach out and say, "I can't believe I had that thought," or "I wonder where my dog is," then we have the ability to intrude with another vibrational energy and help that soul perceive that there is more [to] existence. But we can't intervene unless we're somehow invited.

Me: What do you mean "invited"?

Erik: Opening up or raising their vibration level.

Me: That reminds me of how it's so very difficult for you spirits to manifest or communicate when we're deep in grief.

Erik: Yes! That's exactly right! When you grieve, your vibrational energy is way too dense for us to get through.

Me: I've read that there are seven planes between the physical plane and the "Source." Are there really? You know, you have the astral planes: seven dimensional planes where the seventh one is the Source. Is that how it is?

Erik (laughing): No!

Me: Okay, so it's not true. I was going to ask what plane you're on, but—

Erik: No, there are layers but lots more than seven.

Me: Cool!

Erik: It would be nice to try to zip it up into a seven-layer cake—

Me: Uh-huh.

Erik: —but there are other dimensions in between that. There's so much more, Mom.

Me: I can imagine. But this book I'm reading, called *The Lightworker's Way*, says that Gandhi is on the sixth level, Mother Teresa is on level six, and so on.[3] The astral plane is the first one after the physical plane. But I get the idea that there might not be distinct levels like there are in the seven-layer cake you mention. It's probably not levels the way we conceptualize it as in physical, three-dimensional space.

Erik: You're right! And there's really no way, using your language, to describe it.

Me: So, what dimension are you from, Erik? Mother Teresa lived on Earth, but she was even a sixth-dimensional being, here supposedly.

Erik: Yep, there are people on Earth who live in a higher dimensional plane but reside in the three-dimensional body.

Me: Uh-huh. So, what dimension are you from, Erik, if you could divide it up into seven planes?

Erik: Um, it's not really what you're from; it's what you're in, because where you're from would not really have a relation to who you are.

Me: Okay. Well, that makes sense [barely!].

[Jamie listens to Erik for a few seconds, and then giggles.]

Jamie (to Erik): Can you do that, really? Five and a half?

Me: Oh, okay! So you're really way up there! What dimension am I on? I know I'm not always on Earth—I'll tell you that!

[Jamie giggles.]

Me: God, I'm somewhere else half the time. I think I'm double-parked in the Twilight Zone.

Jamie (still laughing): He puts you at four and a half.

Erik: The Twilight Zone—you wish that existed, Mom! That's somewhere between your café lattes and sleep!

[I laugh in agreement.]

Me: So, I guess when I banished you to the time-out chair all those times, I was pulling rank on you!

[Erik laughs.]

Me: Do you have to be deceased, or in the spiritual realm, to be on some of those higher planes, or—

Erik: Okay, people pass through several planes once they cross over. I'm pretty sure the Earth is on the third-dimensional plane, so there are places of higher vibrations and places of lower ones.

Me: I can't imagine lower ones than Earth. The lower ones are pretty heavy! What's the top plane called?

Erik: I'd call that the Source.

Language and Communication

Erik explained that communication with us is difficult because our language is sequential while that of spirits in the afterlife is not. But I wanted to learn more about the way spirits communicated and the language they used.

Me: Do they have a universal language where you are, Erik? I mean, how do souls speak over there?

Erik: It's kinda the same as telepathy, but it has to do more with feeling what's being said. Feelings are energy based and we are energy, so—Oh, and our mouths don't move.

Me: Oh!

Erik: Well, of course not! It's not like we have real lips and vocal cords and stuff! We don't need that. There's a lot to say about—oh, let me just show you.

[Long pause]

Jamie: Ah! That was a really cool visual. Um, if you can, imagine a person standing in a room, and all of their thoughts and words and how they feel are rotating around them, almost like a solar system, so that, when another person walks up to them, all of the information is accessible. It doesn't have to be translated.

Erik: Yeah, it's like information is coded in energy; information is energy and vice versa. So, since we're all energy, including you guys, all that information is accessible, but it's more freely accessible between

souls over here. How do you think psychics or clairvoyants communicate or tap in to the past or present? How does it happen that someone
in the car next to you at a stoplight senses when you're watching him
pick his nose, and then turns to look at you? It can be felt, merged with,
communicated about in many different ways. But telepathic—Well, I
guess that's the best way I know how to explain it, Mom.

Me: What does the language sound like?

Erik (chuckling): It's not really a sound, Mom. It's soul recognition.
It's instantaneously felt. Think of spirit travel on Earth: we think about
where we want to go and we arrive [there].

Me: Uh-huh.

Erik: Well, if we want to know something, and our vibrational level is
at the height where we can understand it, we think of it and we know.
Then those spirits that tap into our field get that communication. We
don't read a language; we don't communicate in long, extended conversations. We do have sound, though. We're not silent energy; we have
tones and pitches and sounds and languages of all kinds, but everything is understandable. *Everything.*

Me: What about the Akashic Records?

Erik: Those are records where everything—all information—is docu-
mented visually in one language.

Me: Okay. Why?

Erik: It's really archaic. We don't need to have written [languages]. We
access energy to get information, but somewhere along the line of
being human and evolving, written word was present. Hence, docu-
mentation began.

Jamie (chuckling): "Hence"? Really, Erik? *Hence?*

[Erik chuckles.]

Erik: So, really, that's kind of a human thought, a human decision.

Me: Okay. That's interesting. So, is that how you know everything, Erik? Is it like a web that you tap in to—like an energy web?

Erik: Yeah, and it's not like it's above you or below you, Mom. It's not something that constrains you or contains you. It just exists, and you can bring the awareness in your body—your spiritual body—and be calm, and absorb the information you're looking for. It's very gentle. It's easy; it's not abrupt. It's not "in your face," you know?

Me: Yeah, I understand.

Erik: It only comes when you're willing to receive it. And a lot of people—

Jamie (in mock frustration): He's chatty! Slow down, Erik!

Erik: A lot of people, when they die, they don't know how to do that, and they don't wanna know. So they stay in the lower vibrations.

Me: It seems like it's all about matching vibration levels.

Erik: Yep.

The Evolution of the Afterlife

Now that I view the afterlife as dynamic, particularly in the way it's influenced by belief systems, I wonder if it changes or evolves over "time" from a collective perspective.

Me: Erik, does the afterlife evolve after we do? I understand what you've said about how the afterlife evolves for us as individuals, but what about as a collective? I mean, do they have computers there now?

Erik: No.

Me: There are no computers?

Erik: Mom, we *are* the computers. The whole afterlife, the whole universe, every dimension in the universe—and I mean *every* dimension in every universe—is made of information. Waves of information.

Me: Whoa, that's really fascinating! So, what was the afterlife like for the cavemen and cavewomen when they died? As humankind evolves, what happens to the afterlife?

[Long pause]

Jamie: He's getting somebody to help him. Erik was mentioning earlier that, where he is, everything moves like music.

Me: Hm! How nice.

Jamie: But the way he said it had such an incredible visual with it. So everything goes in harmony; everything moves like music. Nothing bumps against anything else; nothing defies the existence of anything else. He says that everything that is, *is.*

Me: Okay.

Jamie: That's my new favorite sentence!

Me: Yeah, I like that! Over here, right and wrong bump into each other, so I can understand how nice that must be over there.

Jamie (savoring each phrase): "Everything moves like music"; everything's in harmony. That's my favorite sentence!

Me: Yeah, I like that!

Jamie: Um, there's a very large gentleman in here now.

Me (jokingly): Oh, maybe it's a caveman!

Jamie (laughing): I kinda think of cavemen as more short and broad.

Jamie: This one is going past my door, and I probably have those industrial doors, so they're about six and a half feet tall.

Me: Uh-huh.

Jamie: So, he's easily seven, seven and a half.

Me: Wow, really?

Jamie: Adam. He says his name is Adam. He says that's a simple name, but he says, "You want it to be simple."

[Jamie and I chuckle.]

Jamie: I said, "Okay." So, his name is probably a lot longer.

Me: Oh, yeah, I bet.

Jamie: He says hello to you.

Me: Hello back!

Jamie: He says he's been conversing with Erik. "Er-ikkkk." His consonants are very clear.

[Jamie giggles.]

[Long pause as Jamie listens to Adam speak.]

Jamie: So, the question was, uh, what did cavemen see when they died?

Me: Uh-huh.

Jamie: He says that life on Earth at that time was still considered new. God's Source had not divided itself in so many ways. It was more pure. Lower vibrations were being experienced and enjoyed—survival, eating, joy in simple ways. And it was a blessing to have it so narrowly focused—not on enlightenment but on survival. That way, God could experience [being God]. Reincarnation was still instated? Hmmmm. I guess he's saying it existed then.

Me: Okay.

Jamie: So, when they passed away, the Light Source would bring them close and then put them back into life on Earth. It was the joy of separation that was the thrill, the excitement—the joy of separation and growing outside of the Light Source.

Jamie (to Adam): So, "Light Source" and "God Source," are those interchangeable for you?

Jamie: Yes. He calls it "Light Source," but he knows our terminology is the word "God."

Me: Oh, okay.

Jamie: He says [the] Light Source expands to other life-forms as well. It's not just based on Earth.

Me: Yeah. That makes total sense. You know, how "God" is dividing and experiencing Itself, evolving just like the pool of consciousness or whatever is evolving too.

Jamie: He smiles really big, sorta boy-like.

Me: Well, Adam, thank you!

Jamie: Aw, he bows his head; he says you're welcome, and he says he will continue to be at your disposal—yours and Erik's.

Me: Aw, well, thank you, Adam!

Jamie (chuckling): He waves to Erik. Erik says, "Thanks!"

What Is Really "Real"?

After gaining so much information about the afterlife, I was left wondering which is real: life here on the earthly plane or life where Erik now lives. Or is everything an illusion created by us—sentient energy that is self-aware and that can create any reality it wants?

Me: We consider a large part of incarnate life to be an illusion. We know that people who leave the incarnate life go home and have an afterlife experience based on their beliefs and expectations—like, hellfire, brimstone, purgatory, and so on—and we know these are illusions. Is Heaven an illusion too? Is it all an illusion? You say you make anything you want: pizza, flat-screen televisions, whatever. Is all that just another form of illusion, like on the earthly plane? Ugh, I'm going around in circles. Sorry. Just, um, is everything in creation an illusion?

Erik (laughing): No, not everything can be an illusion. You have to have a home base. Gotta have the real to balance the illusion.

Me: Okay. So Heaven is not an illusion, but we create illusions or illusory elements within it?

Erik: Everything is real in what some call Heaven. Like, the people who create an image of Hell for themselves, there is no Hell per se, but they will be able to create the fire and brimstone they talk about in religions. But the Hell is a personal one for them. It isn't the one where judgments and damnations are passed. The only illusions are on the earthly plane.

Me: Anything else you want to say about the afterlife, Erik?

Erik: Oh, we can be on this subject all day, Mom.

Me: Well, since we don't have all day, can you just give me one more thing?

Erik: Nothing is fixed. Everything is in existence because it's believed in, not because it's been created by one person.

Me: Okay.

Knowing that place where Erik lives brings me comfort. He's happy, he's thriving, he's cared for. In the end, the afterlife seems to have few differences from the physical world we reside in. There, we have no bodies and we can create reality with our thoughts more instantaneously. But those appear to be the only major differences.

9

SOULS

In this section, Erik expands on the aspects of the soul itself. Some of the questions he answers include: Does reincarnation exist? Do souls evolve? Are souls born, then age, and then die? Do they evolve in the afterlife in the same way they do on the earthly plane? Erik also addresses specific soul types: those of children, of near-death experiencers, and more. What happens to them? How are they treated? This is only a glimpse at a huge amount of information Erik divulges to help us better understand who we really are in the grand scheme of life and the universe.

Reincarnation

Me: When do souls enter the body—at conception, at birth, or all of the above?

Jamie (giggling): He said, "D, all of the above!"

Erik: It's some spirits' lesson to start from the beginning, to transition into the cellular development of a fetus. So, their process starts long before conception.

Me: Oh, wow!

Erik: Yeah, [they do this] because they have to work their way down—work their vibration down to a human vibration, a cellular vibration. It's very pure, very clean, but it's a hard achievement. Most spirits I've seen ride sidesaddle.

[Jamie giggles hard at Erik's description.]

Jamie: That's such a funny visual. He says they ride sidesaddle on the mother's belly until the baby is, um—not fully developed but mostly developed, so that the spirit can merge.

Erik: There are rare occasions when the baby is born and the spirit is not fully attached; that can happen. But mostly, um—

[There is a long pause. I guess at this point, Erik has decided not to finish his sentence. Spirit ADHD!]

Me: I guess it can happen anytime during that process. So, when they're babies, can they just come in and out of the body whenever they want?

Erik: Yes, as babies, as infants. What we call "dream state," where you can change your focus and just project your imagination, your intent—that's an out-of-body experience for a child. They can go in and out of the body much easier than a teenager or an adult can. Then, when people get really, really old, a lot of times they can do that same thing a lot easier than they could before.

Me: It's like they're gearing up to go home.

Erik: Yeah, something like that.

Me: Now, what does it feel like to reincarnate back into a body? Do you go to sleep first? How does it feel? I bet it feels the way I feel trying to get back into my so-called skinny jeans after the holidays. I have to tug on the belt loops and jump up and down!

[Jamie and Erik both laugh hard. I'm sure Erik has seen me get red in the face as I struggle to wiggle into jeans like this. A girl just can't get any privacy, can she?]

Erik: That's a hard question to answer, because you're being specific to one person. The experience is different for everyone. But in general, it does feel like a sleep. I don't know how to describe it except that it's like a simplifying moment. Plus, it depends on how you're reincarnating. Are you coming in at conception; or are you coming in at four months, six months, eight months, or at birth? That makes a big difference in how you need to adjust your spirit to fit the vessel.

Me: On the subject of reincarnation, do animals come back as animals, plants come back as plants, and humans come back as humans, or—

Erik: Animals have a soul a lot like a person does, so when one is attracted to certain animals, there is a significance there. It's all energetic; it's all energy. So, they can come back as an animal or they can come back as a person. If you find yourself drawn particularly to an animal—almost understanding that animal, such as a horse whisperer—you were probably, at one time, that species.

Me: Okay. So, I was never a cockroach. It's official.

Life Cycle of Souls

As humans, we are born, we live, and we die. Everything follows a predictable sequence. Because of this, it's easy for us to assume that every other living being, regardless of which dimension it's in, has a sequential lifecycle as well. But since assumptions have always gotten me into a lot of trouble, I decided to ask Erik about the birth and death of untethered souls and whether either occurred in the first place.

Me: Is the individual spirit ever born in the Source, or has it always existed? How far back into time can that spirit remember?

Erik: Individual spirits are not born. They are just a—

Jamie (to Erik): Do it. Just explain it.

[Pause]

Jamie (to Erik, laughing): No, I don't think there's a word for that, either! He said, "I want a word that means piece—like 'a piece of,' but you're still a part of it." He was telling me how blank the English language can be. I said, "Just explain it out," and he said, "Okay."

Erik: The human spirit is never born. It's just a piece of the whole.

Me: Right.

Erik (sounding a little frustrated at his loss for words): [It's like a] hologram. I don't know anything else that does this—where you can shatter it and pick up all the pieces, and look at the individual piece and there's still an image of the whole. So, Prime Source, God Source, Life Force, whatever the fuck you wanna call it, we are little particles of that whole. Though we identify ourselves in the human form as separate, we're not. We're a part of the whole; we're connected. It's just in subtle energy layers that we don't see. A lot of us can feel them, but most of us cannot see them. So, we aren't really born, because the whole Prime Source, or whatever, has always existed. As far back as you can remember? Um, that's up to you. If—

Jamie (laughing): You know paddleball?

Me: Oh, yeah.

Jamie: It has that elastic string and a rubber ball at the end, and you try to hit it.

Erik: You know a kid version—it has a short elastic string, and it's much easier to do. But you get the adult one, or a cheap one where the elastic is already four feet long, and you can't even swing the ball because the elastic is so long.

Me: Oh, God. I can't even use the kid one.

Erik: Okay, so the ball is the human spirit, and the paddle is the Life Force, God Source.

[Jamie giggles at whatever Erik is now saying.]

Erik: And the string, the elastic, is the subtle energy that keeps us all whole and connected. Sometimes, when you pull away from the God Source, your elastic's really short, and you still have an intense connection and memories. And those memories can go far back—

Jamie (giggling): Um, he's cussing.

Me: Uh oh.

Jamie: The word he wants to use is "beginning," but he refuses to say it, because it's not accurate.

[Jamie and I both laugh at his conundrum. Poor Erik.]

Erik: But in our linear world, that's what we would call it. "Beginning."

Jamie: He's yelling at me, "That's not the right word!" and I tell him, "I know, but you can't come up with another word, can you?"

Me: Oh, he's stumped!

Jamie: Yes. It's ticking him off! Wow. Sore spot!

Erik: Yes! Language is a sore spot for me. It's stupid. I wish I could, you know, just close my eyes, and if you felt it, you'd get it.

Me: I can feel it, but I can't type that [on the blog]. But I can feel what you're talking about, Erik.

Erik: Not linear, but what you'd call back to the beginning. Because you are part of God Source, you have all of the experiences and memories of what God has.

Me: It's almost a *place* instead of a timeline, right?

Erik: Yeah. Yes, yes, yes, yes, yes! And some of us, we have that really long elastic cord, and we just wanted to get as far away as possible, just 'cause it was what we wanted to do. And nobody judged us for it. We just did it, and sometimes it's just hard to get the ball back to the paddle.

[Jamie bursts out laughing.]

Me: Okay, so can you remember the time of the split from the Source?

Erik: Hell yeah!

Me: Wow! What does it feel like?

Erik: I can only speak for myself on this one.

Jamie (laughing): He's going to get all Zen on you!

Me: What?

Erik: I'm going to get all Zen on you.

Me (chuckling): Okay. Got it.

Jamie: I'm just laughing, because the way he said it was so unnatural [for him]. It's funny. He's got his elbows on his knees, and he's leaning forward.

Erik: It's like when the raindrop leaves the cloud. That's how it feels.

Me: Oooh! Wait, how does that feel? I'm not a raindrop, and I'm not a cloud.

Erik: Maybe you should be, Mom.

Mom (laughing, in jest): Oh, God, you little twerp. If so, I just might rain on your parade. So explain.

Erik: Well, it really doesn't have feeling. It's not exciting or scary or anything. It's not like giving birth or painful or—

Me: Is it like a breath?

Erik: Yeah, like when you breathe out—you know, the air that leaves your body as easily as it came in. I hate to disappoint you, but there are no fireworks.

Me: Well, I wouldn't call it disappointing. You might hurt the Source's feelings, you know.

Erik (laughing): No, I'm not! The Source does not judge!

Me: I'm teasing, silly.

Me: How are new souls created—or are they? I suppose they could have always existed, without having a starting point.

Erik: I don't know the answer to this one, so let me ask your guides.

[Pause]

Erik: Okay, okay. Here's what I got from them: They say new souls are created by the all-powerful entity you guys sometimes call "God," the Source, the Light. They're showing me that where you have an existing soul, it can split and split and split into more and more souls, which are the offspring of that single soul. God, or the Source, facilitates this.

Me: Okay. And who decides when that's going to take place?

Erik: The all-powerful Source.

Me: Does this all-powerful being keep creating new souls?

Erik: Yes.

Me: Is there going to be a time when the all-powerful being, He or She or It, stops creating souls?

Erik: Well, that's a time question, but the short answer is no, not to my knowledge.

Me: So it's almost like the branching out of tendrils or tentacles? That's what I'm seeing.

Erik: It looks exactly like that. If you can, try to imagine a beam of light being like a newly fertilized egg; it breaks into two parts, then three, then four. It's the Source breaking off one soul, when the time is right, into one other soul, two other souls—

Me: Does that original soul have anything to do with our parallel lives?

Erik: No, each soul takes on a different personality and a different level of enlightenment.

Me: Ah! So, each soul does not start off at the level of enlightenment of the soul it came from?

Erik: No. It's like when humans give birth. Are [the kids] exactly like the parents? Hell no!

Me: Oh, interesting! Okay.

Erik: And each [soul] stands alone. Also, new souls will come from each [of these] souls as they mature.

[Having lost Erik once, I couldn't bear the thought of losing him again. What if souls could be destroyed? What if they could die? With a great deal of trepidation, I press forward with questions.]

Me: When the United States dropped the H-bombs on Hiroshima and Nagasaki, many, many people died in those blasts. How can a soul possibly survive such an assault when everything around him or her is vaporized?

Erik: You're making it sound like we're comparing the soul to the body—like a piece of glass that is breakable. The soul is not breakable.

Me: Okay. So, the soul can never be destroyed?

Erik: No. The only thing the soul can do is surrender and be absorbed into the main Source. That would be the ultimate disappearance.

Me: Okay.

[Not sure if I like that idea where Erik's concerned.]

Erik: But it's not demanded, and it's not the same as enlightenment— you know, merging with the Source through ultimate enlightenment. That's different.

Me: Do you lose your individual consciousness when that happens?

Erik: Yes.

Me: Oh, boy, that's not good. I don't ever want to lose my sense of self, and I certainly don't want to lose you and your Erik-ness.

Erik: But Mom, you still know who you are, plus you gain the entire mass consciousness. You're just not as separated. It's hard to explain, because it hasn't happened to me. I'm just telling you what I've heard.

Me: I just have this thing about losing that sense of self. It's like dying.

Erik: Mom, from what I understand, it's not like that. It's just so hard to explain it in terms of human language. And back to your question about whether the soul gets vaporized—a soul's energy can get, well, sort of torn by certain traumas. I don't know how to explain it better than that, but as you know, we have healers here that mend energy and make it whole again.

Me: Did you have to have your soul mended since your death was so traumatic and violent?

Erik: Not really. I left my body before the bullet even entered my skull. I did have to go through some therapy to get oriented, to help me fully understand, and to connect my past lives with the emotional issues I had in my last lifetime.

[I remembered that from a previous session.}

Me: Well, is there ever a time when we lose our unique personality when we're fully evolved, and we suck back all those tendrils of our various selves into the Source? Is Erik gone forever when that happens?

Erik: Look, Mom, when you choose to go back to the Source, if that's where you want to be, then you gain the consciousness of everything, like I said. You'll still have the memories of yourself, like, I'd still have my Erik memories, but you'll be completely in God's presence in—

Jamie to Erik (giggling): "The Main Man"—really, Erik? Did you really say that?

[Jamie and I laugh.]

Erik: Not to snub the ladies or anything.

Me: Yeah, what about "The Main Lady"?

Erik: I'm just using a phrase!

Me: So, you get the best of both worlds, is that what you're saying? Or when you go back to the Source, do you have to sacrifice some sense of self?

Erik: Well, you sort of sacrifice a sense of self, because there's no independent action you can perform when you go back to the Source, 'cause you *are* the Source. But you don't really lose your self-identity. There's no loss; there's only gain. If you want to walk back to the God Source, you relinquish your right to be a reincarnating soul. You're a part of the Source.

Me: The collective pool.

Erik: Yes. It's like the comparison of you being alone versus one of many in a school. You're still the personality, Elisa, but you're also part of the whole collection of classmates, the entire school.

Me: Can you change your mind and leave that collective pool, like play hooky from school?

Erik: Sure, nothing is permanent here. Free will reigns throughout.

Me: So, you can definitely get back out—like, separate yourself away from the Source?

Erik: Well, anything's possible, but usually, when you return, that's the ultimate place you wanna be.

Me: Okay, so it's like having a blast in an indoor amusement park and it's storming outside. Why would anyone want to leave the park and stand out in the rain?

Erik: Exactly. But to clarify, a soul never loses its unique personality; we all contribute to the whole. Mom, we're the parts *and* the whole, like a hologram.

Me: Oh, okay. Yeah!

Erik: It isn't about everything becoming One; it's about many different souls evolving to the same level at their own pace. But each one has a very unique personality and very unique experiences. So, they can become a whole that is a much more enlightened whole than it would be if everyone were carbon copies of each other. The uniqueness of the parts is very, very important to the enlightenment of the other parts and the whole. The whole is much greater than the sum of its parts.

Me: Oh!

Erik: And souls never wear out or age. They mature, but they don't wear out or age.

[Of course, my first thought was, "You could have fooled me. My soul feels like it's been trampled by a herd of startled buffalo."]

Me: Good, good. So they don't age unless they want to?

Erik: Yes. Now, we gain knowledge and information, but we don't age; we don't grow old or weak.

Me: But you can choose the age you want to appear as, obviously. Erik, you probably look like you're twenty, twenty-one, but you know, you could just as easily appear as eighty or ten.

Erik: Yes, yes.

Me: So you can raise children; you can have these marriages, so to speak, and you can have children, though not based on biological reproduction, of course. Tell me about that. How is that different than the Source splitting off souls?

Erik: From what I know about that, if a soul decides it wants to experience pregnancy over here, it can.

Me: Hmm! I've had six pregnancies, and all I can say is, "God, who would wanna do that?"

Erik: What a lot of souls will do is just manifest an infant or a small child.

Me: Wow, is it really a true soul?

Erik: Yes, yes! It's another soul in the afterlife.

Me: Huh? But if the God Source is the one responsible for creating new souls, how does that work? How can we manifest a baby?

Erik: Oh, there are always souls hanging around, wanting to be mothered or fathered. A lot of 'em like to be nurtured in the afterlife and on the earthly plane.

Me: Oh, so they can be like an existing soul, not a brand new one!

Erik: Yeah, that's right.

Me: But I guess it's possible to have a brand new soul if the Source breaks off a new one. And then you manifest the infant form for it, right?

Erik: Correct.

Me: Very interesting. Very cool, Erik!

Erik: Let's talk more about the idea of a new soul. Frankly, we're not new at all, because we all come from the God Source, and God ain't new.

Me: Are you saying God's getting a little long in the tooth?

[Erik and Jamie laugh.]

Erik: But if you're asking in terms of whether or not the soul is coming to Earth for the first time—

Me: Or maybe just when the soul individuates or separates from the Source. Hell, I don't really know what I'm asking at all! Help me out here, buddy! Tell me what I'm asking!

[I start laughing at my own confusion.]

Erik: Well, think about it, Mom. We all have [a] conscious, collective memory.

Me: Okay.

Erik: Well, maybe we'll call it a *subconscious*, collective memory. So, the definition of "new" doesn't really fit.

Me: What about a tendril breaking off from the God Source, then? It's still part of the old stuff, but it's new from the standpoint of being a tendril, right?

Erik: Yeah. 'Cause even if a soul is having its first experience, it's not new. So maybe we can ask whether there are still spirits that are having first-time experiences on Earth.

Me: Okay.

Erik: We can say yes, yes there are. The population is growing. But you think, at the same time, look at the rate of trees being cleared. These are all souls coming back to the Source. And of course, there are souls that want to come in. These souls can take the shape of man, of animal—we're really outgrowing ourselves.

Me: Wow, so I'll ask this one again: do animals always come back as animals, a plant as a plant, and a rock as a rock?

Erik: No, that's like saying a black person can only come back as a black person. We're not confined to race.

Jamie: Oh. So Erik, you're putting insects, animals, trees, and humans all on the same level, and you're considering these almost like different races?

Erik: Yeah!

Me: Okay. So, these new tendrils from the Source are being projected to Earth because it sort of accelerates God's experience of Itself?

Erik: Yep.

Me: Because we have more bodies to—

Erik: To fill.

Me: Say an entire family dies in a car wreck. Can the parents live with their children and raise them?

Erik: Yes, Mom. I know what you're saying, and yes. You can maintain that family unit, and you can play life just as you did on Earth.

Me: Okay.

Erik: The only weak moment I can think of is when a person dies on Earth—infant, child, teenager, adult, elderly, or whatever—

Jamie (giggling): He's going through all the ages for us!

Erik: So, at any age, there's that weak spot when they arrive and they go. You know, "I might know where I am, but how does this work? What am I doing?"

Me: Yeah.

Erik: And that's when we band together, and we say, "Let me show you; let me walk you around; let me open your mind."

Me: I see.

Erik: But we're only able to do as much as they're willing to accept or even listen to, and when it gets over their head, it stops right there.

Me: It reminds me of how kids all have to figure things out for themselves—make the same mistakes we made at their age—because they don't want to listen to the advice that comes from our own experience. Reinventing the wheel.

How Souls Evolve after Death

As humans, the influences from our experiences and other people are crucial to how we evolve. But do spirits in the afterlife evolve too? If so, what does that evolution involve? Erik shares his insight.

Me: Does it take some time for the deceased to get used to changing from earthly time to timelessness, and to the change from human emotions to whatever emotions untethered souls have?

Erik: Yeah. Yes, yes, yes.

Me: Yeah, it must be weird. What does it feel like to change from earthly time to timelessness?

Erik: Actually, that's kind of easy, because it's not something that you're really thinking about right away. So much is going on. It's like going to Disney World or going to Vegas, and you're so entertained and you're so partied out and you're so busy—and there are no clocks anywhere—and then you realize you're hungry [and you wonder], "What time is it?" And so, there's an internal need to know. Anyway, so you check in. And when you pass away, you don't have that hunger that kind of pulls you out of the timeframe. You're working on your life and what happened and your funeral and people in your life and learning and expanding, and then you realize, "Oh, this is just how [time] is!" So that's a little bit easier. The thing that fucks you up—

Jamie (laughing): His face was really funny right there! He's pointing his finger.

Erik: Oh, the thing that fucks you up is how people treat you, and that you constantly feel okay. That will really screw with your head, because you're waiting for the other shoe to fall. You're like, "When is this gonna crash? When's this gonna stop?" And it doesn't! Then you learn to allow yourself to get comfortable with it, and then you'll surprise yourself by how you want to react to other people's shit.

Me: Wait. What?

Erik: Oh, let's say "spirits."

Jamie: Thank you.

Erik: So, another soul walks in, and they have their shit going on, but you get close to them, and normally, as a human, you would—

Jamie (giggling): What?

Erik: Coddle them and all that shit.

Jamie: He's laughing. So, "nurture them," Erik?

Erik: Yeah. Nurture them. All of a sudden, you just don't have that need to do it. It's because you absolutely know that they're okay. There's no internal pull to react—like, as a "good human," you know—because compassion is always done. You don't have to trigger it to arrive. It's pretty cool. I still get surprised by some of the shit I pull off.

[Jamie and I giggle.]

Me: So, what else about the change from human emotions to whatever emotions untethered souls have? Tell me more.

Jamie: He's laughing.

Erik: When you're watching your loved ones on Earth, and they get sad—when you were alive, you'd either feel guilty or you'd go help 'em, like, you'd wanna do something. But now when they get sad, you understand why. You clearly know it's not about something you've done. You instantly know they need to react this way to understand what lesson is coming. And that's pretty cool. But then you start to see that humans are really just emotional beings; like, that's truly the core of what kind of creatures we are. And when you spiritually show up next to your human family, and they emotionally react to you, that's pretty cool; because when you were living and they came into a room, they'd turn and see you, and they'd logically react and say, "Hey, what are you doing. Where are you going?" They wanted to seek your information instead of understanding how you were feeling. That's pretty cool and different. That's why it's sometimes hard when, you know, we get next to our human family and they cry when they feel us—because it reminds them that we're gone.

Me: Uh-huh.

Erik: Sometimes that's more difficult to handle than anything else. We really want them to react by smiling and going, "Ah, I remember the day when he was such an asshole, and I miss him so much!"

[Jamie and I laugh at his unexpected remark.]

Me: Yeah, so you can get sad?

Erik: Yeah. You can get sad, but it's so different. It's not you like sit around with a group of sad souls and converse about it. It's just an inner experience, and it doesn't feed upon itself. Like I've said before, it's really hard to maintain those lower vibrations. It's like keeping a fire alive in the rain. You gotta really work at it to keep it going, keep it going, keep it going. As soon as you, you know, let go of that effort, it's gone. The sadness is gone. Happiness is truly middle ground here.

Me: You say humans are emotional beings and spirits are not humans, but they're still emotional beings, right?

Erik: Absolutely.

How Souls Communicate

Erik explains how spirits communicate in general terms, but how do they communicate with each other?

Me: How do souls like you communicate? Describe it in terms of what we do, what symbols do we, uh— What in the world am I saying here? I just have absolutely no idea! I mean, I know there's telepathy, but do you communicate in chunks of ideas, in symbols? Do you use linear language like we do? What is it? How do you communicate over there?

Jamie (laughing): Erik's looking at me and saying, "What's wrong with this person? Does she have diarrhea?"

Me (firmly): No, Erik, it's my question. So stop it right now, young man.

[We all laugh.]

Me: I can take a swig of Kaopectate if that helps.

Jamie: Oh, my God, he's cracking up.

Me: Sometimes you need it too, Mister Oral Diarrhea. But seriously, how do you communicate with each other? Not with me but with each other? I know that we touched on this a little bit before, but I'd like to know more.

Erik: We don't open our mouths. We don't even have to stand next to each other. It's not called telepathy because it's not a brain-to-brain activity. Think of it more as how a computer system communicates, you know, through the air, bouncing off the satellite dish and then to its directed source. [I thought he meant "target," but he clears this up later.] Think of it more mathematically—that my energetic body, my spirit, once it is thinking or feeling a concept, is being immediately directed to the source of what I'm thinking about or feeling about, and that source is experiencing it simultaneously. By the way, this is no new bullshit because it's exactly how the human body works; it's just on different vibrational levels. But it's exactly how the human body works, and it's exactly how telepathy kind of goes.

Me: And instead of beaming up to the source, we're beaming up to the brain? Is that what you're saying?

Erik: Yes. Yeah, yeah.

Me: Okay.

Erik: Brain-to-brain activity, but there's no satellite dish for us to bounce off of. It bounces off pure source energy. God energy. Life Force energy. That's really what's carrying or motivating—giving motion—to how we communicate. We don't have to call someone and set up a meeting; there's no withholding [information] here. I can't have a thought about you and you not know about it. We're all open books. And even if I had a thought [about you] that you would normally judge as not being good, you would still experience it, but you would have no desire to judge me for it. That's a human quality—the desire to judge and measure and shred things apart.

Me: Yes, unfortunately.

Erik: You would just know that that was my truth, and that's where I was coming from. You wouldn't have a dire need to react emotionally with instantaneous love or disapproval, or whatever. It just is. And that freedom of having no judgment or instant reaction, that's where all of this compassionate—

[Pause]

Jamie: He's looking for a word.

Erik: Amazing space that I exist in right now.

Jamie (chuckling): He looks so unsatisfied that he just used the word "amazing"!

Erik: That's why some people who have those near-death experiences, you know, they don't wanna come back. Even if it means leaving the love of their life behind, or [even if someone] depends on them, they don't wanna come back. They know it's gonna be okay. I don't know whether I explained that right. I fucked up.

Me: Aw, you did fine, Erik. But when you communicate, what is it that goes to the satellite dish, so to speak? Does it come in words, chunks of ideas, symbols?

Erik: No, it's like getting visuals and emotions and verbiage all at once.

Me: Hmm. Confusing. That's called multitasking.

Erik: Nah, it's actually a really clear way 'cause you get the exact emotion that's behind it. You don't have to guess like you do when you read an email. You get to see what the person is creating or thinking, you know, so there's more detail in the visual than there is in just the description in words, and then you get the verbiage that goes with it. And it's not really like English, you know. It's not like Spanish or any other language, either. It's a distinct language. It's just like this core language that you understand, and that's what you communicate in. Even with alien forces, other nations that come [to this dimension], we're able to communicate. We don't need a translator to come here.

Me: Okay, so are you saying that they're words?

Erik: Yeah. They're words.

Me: What do you call the language?

[Pause]

Me: In that language. Say the name of the language in that language.

Jamie: We're having a bit of an argument. He's saying, "I don't fucking know, because it's not like, when you die, you go to school and you learn how to speak this language."

Erik: You just instantly know how to do it. It's just part of you. It's like an emotional language, but it does have words. It's not heavy on labels and conjugation. You don't have to sit down and learn it. It's not a foreign language.

Me: How do you say, "How are you?"

[Long pause]

Jamie (to Erik): No.

Jamie (to me): He looked at me; his eyes got a little bit more wide, and he put his hands out and said, "Did you get it?"

Me (Laughing): Oh!

Jamie: I know, right? The most that I understood was, "I love you."

Me: Aw! So you can speak it, Erik, but we can't receive it.

Jamie (to Erik): Oh, so I got it as an emotion. As love.

Me: Oh!

Jamie: But then I translated it into the words "I love you," instead of just receiving love.

Me: How interesting.

Erik: Yes, because if you're asking how somebody is, you're showing care; you're showing love for them.

Me: All of this is so fascinating. Okay, so what if I say, "How does the universe really work?"

[Pause]

Jamie: Hey, that communication/message actually came from me! Yay!

[I chuckle.]

Jamie: It's easy to receive messages and communicate around Erik now. I got this picture in my head—this picture of complete unity. I still had my own skin, but I was in relation with everything around me, not just the room or the city or the United States or Earth. It was something larger—solar systems and so forth. It looked like an electric spiderweb that had a light source to it. It was intricately woven and very 3-D. It was not like a flat image at all, but I did feel like I was looking at it from an outside source. I wasn't in it, because he was trying to give me the image, but Erik said that, if I tried to hang on to it more, I would have gotten more of the concepts that he was trying to fly by.

Me: Did you get any feeling or emotion along with it, or were you not hanging on long enough?

Jamie: No, the feeling was just complete unity, complete acceptance, that there wasn't anything that was unnatural or out of place or going against the curve.

Me: Ah, that's awesome. Lucky you!

Jamie (chuckling): He pointed at me and said, "That's even about your pain."

[Erik's referring to Jamie's neck pain from a car accident that she had about a year ago.]

Me: What, you're one with your pain? That sucks! You need to pick that one little spiderweb off! Can you do that?

[Jamie laughs.]

Erik: You can peel it off, but you can't destroy it, nor can you change it. If you place it somewhere else, it might be somebody's joy, not somebody's pain. It doesn't always give the same reaction.

Me: Okay. Anything else you want to communicate to us about communication?

Erik (laughing): I love the subject, even though it's hard to translate it well. Humans are kind of stuck in the idea that they have to use their voice to communicate. It's bullshit.

Me: Well, it's hard—it's *really* hard—but I get what you're talking about. I really do, Erik, because when we talk, there are visual and emotional components to our communication. But the person on Earth only receives the words. A certain inflection and tone of voice can translate some of the emotion, but not all of it. And we can describe some of the visuals, but not all of it and not completely. Other people in our lives can't see what we see. So, it's frustrating, even here.

Jamie: He's smirking and nodding his head.

Children's Souls

Children differ from adults for many reasons. For one, when they are very young, they have not been influenced by outside sources and therefore have no preconceived notions. Since our belief systems determine our death and afterlife, I wonder how this lack of influence affects these souls.

Me: Okay, now, Erik. What about children? What is their experience after death, since they really don't have a belief system indoctrinated into them? Can you tell me more about that?

Erik: Well, most of the time, with children, they know they're going to die in advance. There's no fear around it, so their perspective of death is very clear.

Me: That's good.

Erik: Think about it, Mom. Fear is part of a belief system and it clouds our perspective a lot. Fear comes from an expectation of what [death] should be like, and it doesn't happen according to those expectations. That's why some grown-ups are afraid when they first cross over. But with little kids, there is no fear. Fear is the underbelly of belief, Mom.

Jamie: Oh, he gave me a cool visual with that. It was like, I guess an animal belly—like a big fat cow belly—but it was red, like on fire. That was the fear, like the underbelly of belief.

Me: Wow.

Jamie: It was just a quick, cool image.

Erik: So, kids don't have that. They cross with no fear, feeling completely safe.

Me: Oh, that's so good.

Erik: Yeah, I know. They're wide-eyed; they're looking around. The Light is present, and God is felt in everything, everywhere. Who the hell would be afraid of that?

Me: Yeah.

Erik: And then commonly, if they know or recognize a family member, that person will be there. If they're young enough, Mom, they remember the spirits that were there to send them off when they were about to go into the belly. And if they're going because they're not carried to term for whatever reason, that's a very hard lesson to learn. So that baby spirit gets a heads up. They're doing it sometimes to get the lesson themselves on, you know, not being able to complete the process. Or they're really making a true sacrifice. They go through it so that the mother and other family members can have the lesson. In that case, it's often to learn about loss. It's just so different every time. But it's [all] part of the plan.

Me: Makes sense.

Jamie: I've communicated with many, many children who are to depart soon, and it's often children who are ill or terribly injured who are reassuring their older siblings or parents or grandparents that everything's going to be okay. They have a much easier ability to see their guardian angels, to sense, to intuit very plainly and clearly what's happening and why—that it's going to be okay. They're going to end up back in Heaven; they're going to be with their angels; they're going to be with God; they're going to be with other loved ones who are still in the afterlife. And so, they have a very different experience in that, if they have an injury or an ailment, they're often able to pass—not in every single case, but often—very calmly, with the soul passing out of the body. It can be a very pleasant experience, even if they're suffering [from] pain.

Me: Good. That makes perfect sense.

Erik: Now, children who suffer violent deaths, their passing is not as pleasant. In other words, if children feel like they're having more control over their passing, like with an injury or ailment, they have people around them to take care of them generally. But if they have an adult who is abusing them, they suffer until their soul pops out of the body. And then they're like everybody else. The soul joyously returns to Heaven and resumes its life there. It's just not as pain-free a death as when kids die after a period of injury or disease. If the death is sudden, like with a car accident or something, there's not much time to feel any pain.

Me: So, why are kids able to share dreams with us, have imaginary friends—which I'm sure just means they can see and communicate with their spirit guides—and see the deceased more [easily]? Why is that?

Erik: Because the part of the brain that discounts all of that hasn't taken hold yet; [it] hasn't become the dominant, directing force of their being. That's just one reason. After a while, they pick up on the fact that adults don't see spirits as often, so they're like, "What the fuck? Maybe I'm nuts." So, that ability gets suppressed.

Me: Yeah, and is it also because it takes a few years before they totally commit to that body? Does it take time to completely connect and become grounded to their new body?

Erik (laughing): Well, some people never do!

Me (laughing): And I think I'm one of them!

Erik: Ha! Yeah. Some people never get comfortable in the body, and they see the earthly plane as totally alien, and being in a physical body as alien.

Me: Yep, yep.

Erik: And guess what? It is! We spend most of our time here in Heaven, in spirit.

Me: Yep, that's true! So why is it that, when we become adults, we stop being able to see spirit? Why wouldn't it totally be okay for us to see *you*, say? What's wrong with us humans being able to see all spiritual beings?

Erik: But Mom, you can!

Me: I know, I know, but why isn't it easier? Why isn't it as easy as me looking at the toaster on the kitchen counter? Why can't it be as plain as day—like you walk through the front door in plain sight and say, "Hey Mom, I'm home!"

Erik: But it can be.

Me: Aw, I was afraid you'd say that. I haven't been able to have that experience—yet.

Erik: If a spiritual being chooses to materialize, and if a human being works on their ability to receive electrical energy, it can be that way, Mom. That's all I got. You know spiritual beings vibrate at a higher frequency, right?

Me: Yeah, so you've said.

Erik: And that frequency is not in the visible part of the electromagnetic spectrum—I mean the visible part for humans. So, like I've said before, we have to lower our frequency, and you have to raise yours to get the visual manifestation you're looking for. Back to kids and their special abilities—it's the same as when we die. It takes time for our humanness to wear off—to adjust to our new positioning and to remember our abilities. We talked about this transitional phase before. Same with kids. They get born, and it takes time for them to adjust to their new, narrow-minded, lower-vibrational existence.

Jamie (chuckling): He says it with such a dull voice, like monotone.

Me: You sound like Ben Stein, Erik!

Erik: Here's another thing: kids now are coming down [to Earth] with these spiritual memories, because they're helping with the evolution of the earthly plane. And these kids won't completely lose their memory of how to communicate with the spiritual realm. It'll be common for them.

Me: Oh, good! But before, we indoctrinated the spiritual abilities and memories right out of them by saying things like, "There are no such things as imaginary friends!"

Erik: Yes, Mom. Exactly. But now that more parents have had these same experiences, they look at their child with a new respect.

Me: Good!

Erik: And it's changing from "A child should be seen and not heard" to "A child should be heard—and respected."

Me: Yeah, absolutely. Okay, since we make life plans and contracts before incarnating, before that incarnation, a spirit clearly isn't a baby. Why is it that, when they cross back over, they're still babies? It doesn't make sense to me, especially since there's no time there anyway. So, I guess, when a baby dies, they go to Heaven—or the other side or whatever you want to call it—and they're still a baby, even though they've been grown-ups in many other past lives? How does that work?

Erik: Okay, look, there are a few ways this can play out. Let's say a family loses their child at age two, and the child doesn't want to reincarnate; the child wants to stay with the family and continue its path of growing up. The child limits itself to behave like a human and grow up [in the same way as its earthly family].

Me: Ah! I see.

Erik: So, it still serves as a missing link to the family, though not in a physical body. There are times when the child passes over and reincarnates back into the family or into another family, and so, for that original family, it's like a snapshot in history: the child is two years old; the child will always be two years old. Their previous family members have dreams, and the child shows up as two years old. God, Mom, there are so many ways, depending on the needs of the family involved and the actual soul involved!

Me: All right. So they can grow up over there if they choose to, but they can also just, you know, be the same age as when they passed.

Erik: Yeah, and when they pass over, they can adopt their thirty-year-old body from a previous life. They're pure energy. Their appearance really means nothing to them in terms of who they are, but it means everything to you all there on Earth.

Me: Ah!

Erik: And there are a lot of times—

[Jamie listens.]

Jamie: Is that true, Erik?

[Jamie listens some more.]

Jamie: That was through you? Bradley—really? I'm going to look this up.

Me: What are y'all talking about?

Jamie: Well, I had a reading this week, where a woman wanted to communicate with her grandson—

Me: Uh-huh. Wait, you mean Brady? The little boy who was—

Jamie: Rolled over on, yeah.

Me: She's one of the blog members!

Jamie: Yes, okay. I spoke with her this week, and Erik is saying that, with Brady, um, he died very young, just a few months old.

Me: Uh-huh.

Jamie: And now, when you look at Brady, he's about three years old.

Me: Okay.

Jamie: And the reason he's adopting the form of a three-year-old is so he can kind of "count down," because he's going to be coming back into that family, through the same mom, in about three years. So by adopting that age, he's going to "grow down" and prepare again to create his body, and then come out.

[Jamie and I chuckle.]

Me: So it's like three years from now for Brady in the afterlife? Is that what you're trying to say, Erik?

Erik: Yeah.

Me: Very cool!

Nonhuman Souls

I have always adored my cats and dogs. When they have died and crossed into their afterlife, I've wondered if they will be there to greet me when I cross over. I also wanted to know how their souls differ from those of humans.

Me: Are our pets, or better said, our animal companions, with us when we pass?

Erik: Yes!

Me: Ah, interesting! Wow! So our animal companions are with us. Are fish and other animals that are there in the afterlife a product of our thoughts, or are they separate forms of consciousness that have crossed over?

Erik: They are each souls.

Me: Oh, okay. So it's not like we create the fish that we catch if we go fishing [in the afterlife]. They are separate souls.

Erik: Yes.

Me: Do animals ever reincarnate into humans and vice versa? Same for plants and rocks—are these interchangeable when it comes to reincarnation?

Erik: Yeah. Now, think about it, Mom. If you think that is a weird answer, then you're placing judgment that you are better than a rock.

Me: Oh! Well, yeah, I see what you mean.

[Note to self: search the internet for rescue pet-rock adoptions.]

Erik: There's no life force out there that is better or worse than the other, and so, yes, there is exchange. There can be a human-like soul and intelligence within the animal companion or in the tree in your front yard.

Me: Ah! So Erik, you can come back as a tree if you want to?

Erik (chuckling): Yeah!

Jamie (giggling): He's got his eyebrows way up!

Me: Or can you sort of put part of your soul into a tree, and then—

Erik: Yes, and then still be alive, spirit-wise, to communicate and be who I am!

Me: Yeah? Wow! Can you do that as a dog too—like can an animal companion have a piece of human soul in it?

Erik: Yes, but Mom, to say "a piece" suggests that it's part of a whole. When we divide, even the divided parts are all complete; they're all whole. Remember, it's like a hologram.

Me: Yeah.

Erik: So we've gotta be wise when we choose our vocabulary.

Me: Exactly.

Erik: 'Cause even when we divide, we divide into complete pieces.

Me: So, it doesn't mean "Erik" is cut in half; it's like now there are two Erik souls.

Erik: Right, and each part is just as powerful as the next. Getting back to your example, when my life as an animal companion ends, then that soul merges with the one I already have. We all come back together. It's not like we divide and keep expanding and dividing.

Near-Death Experiences

Me: What happens energetically when a soul has had a near-death experience and then comes back into the body?

Erik: That's when the soul doesn't separate from the physical body.

[Long pause]

Jamie: Sorry. He's giving images.

Erik: There is an out-of-body experience, and they travel dimensionally back Home. They're allowed to journey and see what's going on. But because it's not the best and appropriate moment for them to be deceased, they are guided back to the body and pushed back in.

Jamie: Nice. "Pushed back in." Shoved.

Me: Like Japanese commuters when they're shoved into the subways. Not comfortable!

[Jamie laughs.]

Me: Hey, get back in there! But they're still attached on a cellular level, right?

Erik: Yeah, right.

Me: So, when they travel to the other dimension, to Home, their soul is attached to other cells. . . . I don't get that visual.

Erik: The soul leaves the body, but it doesn't become a spirit. It's kind of how you have an out-of-body experience. The only difference between an out-of-body experience and a near-death experience is that there is a [medical] team, there is someone who is measuring the physical body and stating that the heart is no longer beating, the breath is no longer occurring. So, [the person is] pronounced dead. But there is a cord and connection, and that connection to the body is not released.

Me: And with the out-of-body experience, you obviously still have the vital signs, and there's still a cord, but is the soul is connected on a cellular level in both cases. That's what I'm trying to understand. How are they connected to the cells?

Erik: In the case of an out-of-body experience, the soul is always connected to each cell. But in the case of an NDE, it actually depends on what kind of trauma or stress the body is in. If the body is deprived of oxygen, then there's already a chemical reaction that the body is going through, [which causes] the energy to pull out. If it's a bleed out, it's different. If it's, you know, trauma to the head, that's different too. You know, the chemical process in the body will help dictate which cells are going to stay in contact with the soul and which cells aren't. But overall, if you want less detail, you explain it this way: even in the near-death experience, you still have a cord; you're still corded to the body.

Me: So, only in true death, are you not corded?

Erik: Yeah. You're completely separated. There's no way you're slamming your soul back into your body.

Me: It's like a cell phone—no cord.

Erik: Yup. Cut the cord, but you can still communicate.

Me: Exactly. And I'm so glad.

With each conversation Erik and I had, I grew in my confidence of his voice and of my own growing understanding of the way things work for untethered souls. As I continued on my journey of getting to know Erik as he is now, he began to challenge me with some truly mind-bending material. I began to take notice of how he had oriented himself to his new surroundings and learned how to tap in to the vast web of information available to him. As you will see in part 3, I have learned how he has broadened his view to include larger concepts, such as the nature of consciousness, of time and space, of reality itself, and of much, much more. As I began to ask Erik "bigger" questions, and we continued developing our new relationship across the veil, my skepticism began to erode, leaving in its wake an open, curious mind and an open heart. I've always been proud of my son, but I feel a sense of awe when I think of all he offers to the world now. He has insight. He has wisdom. He is a teacher. In the conversations that follow, I suggest you fasten your seat belt as Erik takes your mind on a roller coaster, the likes of which you've never been on before.

PART III

THE BIGGER PICTURE

10

THE NATURE
OF CONSCIOUSNESS

In my ongoing quest for knowledge and understanding, I have explored various theories about what this thing we call "existence" truly is, and I have asked many questions along the way. For example, what are the origins of consciousness? What is it made of, if anything? How does it relate to our physical form? Is it separate from the mind or a part of it? Is it, in a word, "us"? In my conversations with Erik, I learned that all things have what we call "consciousness"—sometimes self-aware, sometimes not. As humans, we are nothing less and nothing more than self-aware sentient energy. I also learned how consciousness attaches to the physical body on a cellular level of what it is made of. Furthermore, Erik dove into some of the science behind the nature of consciousness, which went a long way in soothing some of the ruffled feathers of the scientist in me.

It doesn't stop there, however. In the conversations to come, Erik describes the consciousness of animals, plants, and inanimate matter as well. For me, these revelations were startling, because they forced me to redefine myself and my environment, living and non-living, and to broaden my understanding of existence yet again. Now, I no longer consider myself a woman with a body, a brain, and a full complement of emotions, all separate from each other. Thanks to my son, I understand that I am much more than that.

What Is Consciousness?

Me: Erik, is the "consciousness" the same thing as the "soul"?

Jamie (giggling): Erik's kind of mumbling. He's like, "That's a good one." He's got his elbows on his knees; he's sitting on the back of my couch. When he thinks, he messes up his hair.

Me (giggling): Oh, yeah, as if it's not messy enough! He used to do that all the time. I think I even have a picture of him doing it.

Jamie: It never really lies down flat!

Me: I know! He's got a couple of cowlicks!

Jamie: Is that why?

Me: Yeah, and he wasn't big on running a comb through it!

Jamie: I thought it was just wavy!

Me: Oh, well, it's wavy too. He's got the best of both worlds. Cowlicks and curls.

Jamie (laughing): So funny!

Erik: Ahem.

[Pause]

Erik: The consciousness is sorta like a branch of the soul, but in itself, defined by itself. Let's say you have a store, and the store is the soul.

Me: Okay.

Erik: The front doors are consciousness. They open and close. Now, the doors are part of the store, but they have their own specific function. That's kinda the idea I wanna convey. Consciousness can open (*poof!*) or close, and when it's closed off, you have the subconscious lying behind it, inside the store.

Me: Interesting. I read something about microtubules in the cells being the origin of consciousness. Is that true, and does consciousness have substance?

[Microtubules are tiny tubes inside cells that have several functions. They maintain cell structure, are involved in intracellular transports, and play an important role in cell division.]

Erik: Well, energy is substance, so yes, it has substance. But science wants that substance to be very low vibration and tangible. Now, these microtubules, they can contain the energy patterns of how the consciousness roots into the physical body, because they're throughout the body in the cells.

Jamie: Oh, are they? What are they? Oh, never mind. I don't need to ask the questions.

Me: No, go ahead! So, you're saying these microtubules aren't the origin of consciousness, but maybe they anchor consciousness to the cells?

Erik: [A microtubule is] a container.

Me: Does it contain the roots of the consciousness so that it connects to the body, or . . . I don't know . . .

[Jamie laughs.]

Erik: Yeah, there are a lot of scientists who believe that the microtubules' hollow space has no purpose in the body, no function. Or when they test these hollow spaces, they see that they have a function they can't define. This is where spirituality and science are gonna come together hand in hand. They're going to start understanding that all energy is matter and all matter is energy, and they're gonna create tools of measurement to find that.

Me: So, microtubules are—

Erik: They're sort of an anchoring system. It's how the soul or consciousness anchors to the physical body.

Me: Okay, here's a question from one of the blog members: "What's the association between the soul, the body, and the mind?"

Erik: Well, that could be taken a few ways. Do they mean the exact physical association, or the energetic association?

Me: Hmm. I don't know. Physical, maybe? Or both?

[Jamie laughs hard at Erik before translating his answer.]

Jamie (to Erik, still laughing): Oh, really? That's not a joke, Erik?

[She continues to laugh until she catches her breath enough to tell me what he said.]

Erik: It's the belly button.

Me: Oh, okay!

Jamie: I was like, "What?"

Me (chuckling): Ah, so that's why you have to contemplate your navel. It's all coming together now! The key to all the answers in the universe come right down to the belly button!

Erik (laughing): Well, everything is connected to the navel. The umbilical cord comes from it; that's the first source of nourishment; that's where the womb [attaches]. Or like in Hinduism, a chakra sits right behind it—the base of the soul.

Me (teasing): Ah, so *that's* why it so important to clean the lint out of our belly buttons from time to time.

Erik: Bingo! Also, the brain is like the storage box that you rent, that gets dropped off in your driveway. You put shit in it. It's still on your property and you're storing nice things in there, but it doesn't run the whole show.

Jamie: So, he's saying, if he had to point to a physical place (where the spirit and body connect,) it'd be the belly of the body.

Me: Okay. What about the energetic association of the soul within the body and mind?

Erik: Energy exchange between body, mind, and soul—this happens at every level, in every cell. Energy exchange of all three happens consistently throughout. There's not a small portion kind of leaking out bits, traveling down an artery or vein, and feeding different areas. It encompasses the entire being, from the intracellular level up.

Me: So, the energetic connection is pervasive between the three?

Erik: Yeah, 'cause remember, it's all energy. Everything is energy—the mind, the body, and the soul.

Me: You make it sound so very easy, sweetie!

Erik: It is, Mom. Everything is very simple, really. It just requires a different way of looking at things.

Neutrinos

Me: Let's talk about neutrinos. It's said that those are the particle of consciousness, that they're the carrier of all information. Is that true? If not, what are the soul and consciousness made of?

Erik: Well, the soul and consciousness—

[Long pause]

Jamie (to Erik): Great imagery, but you have to put it into words for me, Erik.

Erik: The soul and consciousness have to morph to fit into whatever dimension they're in. There's not one single package that works for all dimensions. For the human life, as you mentioned, Mom, it's the neutrino. In spirit it has a different terminology.

[Pause]

Jamie (to Erik): Right, because it can't be a lower vibrational frequency like a physical particle.

Me: So, the neutrino is different in the physical than it is in spirit?

Erik: Yeah.

Me: In what way? Is it more of a wave pattern than a particle pattern there?

Erik: Wave makes me think of sound, but I'm talking in terms of vibration.

Me: Oh, okay. So, it has a higher vibration. And what's important about the neutrino? What makes it special?

Erik: Just like the soul, it's one of the only things that transforms from three-dimensional life into the afterlife. It carries on without getting broken or destroyed, whereas your hair can't do that; nothing on your physical body can do that.

Me: Okay. And they say it can pass though anything, even lead, so that must be why you can pass through walls when you're in spirit. Is that right, Erik?

Erik: Correct.

Me: So, they are the building blocks of consciousness, of the soul. Is that what you're saying?

Erik: Yes.

Me: How does a neutrino function?

Erik: It functions just like the thread. It holds everything together, but there is no hole or gap in existence.

Me: But on the level of the particle itself, how does it work? Does it create some sort of energy, for example?

Erik: No, it's not creating some sort of electrical current. It's more like a glue. It doesn't have information or data in it, but it holds it.

Jamie (to Erik): Okay, that, my friend, did not make sense.

Erik: It doesn't possess energy. It carries it. It creates these glue-like connections and carries information.

Me: Oh. So, it's not information itself.

Erik: No, it's like a transmitter.

Me: Oh, it transmits information?

Erik: Yeah, like, you know, Bluetooth.

Me: Oh!

Erik: Like the Bluetooth in your car.

Me: Oh, I see.

Erik: It doesn't have all of the information, but, through it, you can find all the information.

Me: So, are we the information? Are we sentient energy, so to speak?

Erik: Yes.

Me: It's so interesting, what consciousness is, isn't it?

Erik: Yes. We are information that is self-aware.

Me: And the neutrinos—waves in spirit and particles here—are what carry not only self-awareness, but all of the information that we gather from different lives?

Erik: Bingo.

Me: Wow. So, the neutrino is the Bluetooth technology that gets us all the information we need, including our own awareness of self.

[Erik nods his head.]

Me: Phew! My brain is about to explode. Okay. Then here's one from your dad: "Where in the body does the soul reside and what shape is it? Is it in the head, the heart, or where?" I'm thinking it's probably much bigger than the physical body.

Erik: You're right. It is bigger, because our energy extends beyond the body. You can kind of think about it like an ice cube in water. Same content, right? But the ice is solidified, and then it goes to water, and then it goes to vapor. So, the ice would be the body. The bulk of the soul is in there, and it creeps into every vein, every cell, every fingertip. It's not all bundled up in a head; it's not tucked away behind the heart. It encompasses the whole thing, because then it bleeds out of the skin, changes its shape just a little bit, and creates that energetic field. Then it bleeds out again too—like vapor—and has a different energetic field.

Me: Very cool. Pappa also wanted me to ask this one, and I think it's just so cute: "When you chop off a hand without warning, what happens to that part of the soul that occupied the hand?"

Erik (chuckling): It still exists in the shape of the hand. It still moves like the hand would, and it's still wired to the brain and will receive those signals and behave in that manner.

Me: Oh, that's why you can have phantom limb pain, I guess!

Erik: Absolutely! You got it!

Animal, Vegetable, Mineral

Me: I guess everything has some form of consciousness? Even animals, plants, and inanimate objects?

Jamie: Erik is putting his hands out, saying, "Hellooooo, I know! People forget to ask what happens to plant spirits."

Me (chuckling): Hey, what happened to my beautiful bougainvillea that died in the freeze last year? I wanna know! I had those for twenty years!

Jamie: Oh, poor things.

Me: I know. So everything has some sort of consciousness, then? Even a rock? Do rocks have some form of primitive consciousness?

Erik: Well, yes, but— What has awareness? That's the question I think you're asking, and that would include things that can produce a more complex life-force energy. They need food, they reproduce, they grow. That's where souls are. Rocks and things like that have only a primitive, unaware consciousness. Mom, there are so many different kinds of life forces on the Earth, but for so long, we've been pretending that we're the only ones.

Me: Humans can be so rude!

Erik: I know!

[Jamie listens to Erik as he chatters away at a rate much too fast for her to translate. She then paraphrases what she remembers.]

Jamie: He's talking about these birds that have funerals. I can't keep up with him, he's talking so fast! He's talking about sparrows and crows and blackbirds that bring twigs and cry and place the twigs over their fallen feathered friend.

Erik: This has been happening for centuries; this is not new. We're just finally seeing it. I think what's happening is that humans think they've tapped out on all the new discoveries, right? They've labeled, they've logged everything, so now they can, with their own eyes, see the spirituality that lies within everything that they've labeled.

Me: How does the consciousness of rocks and plants and animals compare to human consciousness? Can you describe these more?

Erik: Well, rocks are different from plants and animals.

Me: Okay.

Erik: Plants and animals have a living source, a life source, like I said. They create food, life energy, um—

[Very long pause. Jamie hums in mock impatience.]

Erik: Describe it?

Jamie: Yeah, like color or shape, whatever.

[Pause]

Jamie (laughing hard): Describe it, Erik!

[Very long pause (This must be a tough one.)]

Jamie: He's trying really hard to gather the words up. He wants to talk about rocks first.

Erik: Rocks and minerals—it's energy that *is*. There's not so much of what you'd call a consciousness, but it does have a primitive and unaware life force in it. Um, plants and animals have a higher, more complex vibrational life force, so it shifts and it grows and it moves.

Me: Interesting!

Erik: So, when we look at [plants and animals], [the energy] has a pulse to it. It has a movement to it, whereas the energy of a rock doesn't have that movement. It's like stagnant energy. Rocks have stagnant energy.

Me: Oh, okay.

Erik: But something like wood, which once was a sustainable life force—you know, before we cut it up, made furniture out of it, and so forth—it contains all the memory from when it was alive; it contains that source. But just as when something dies, it ceases to have movement to it. It becomes energy force that just "is." So, I guess that's the main difference: stagnant versus moving energy.

Me: Wow, I find myself patting my desk here. [to my desk] Oh, I'm so sorry you were cut up! So Erik, I guess plants have feelings, sensory feelings. Do they have emotions?

Erik: Yes! They get happy, they get scared, terrified. They feel pain. When chemicals are put on them, for example, they pull back—their energy pulls back. They communicate to each other by movement and root systems.

Me: Uh-huh.

Erik: They even fight!

Me: Wow! What about animal consciousness compared to that of plants or other vegetation.

Erik: Animals, we can link more to our own personal energy, where they have more of a, um—

[Long pause]

Jamie (chuckling): Yeah, you're going to catch yourself there, Erik, 'cause you've got to use our descriptive words.

Me: Ha!

Jamie: He says that he doesn't mean to say plants are lesser forms of life than people, but I think that's the only way he can put it—that animals have more of a thinking consciousness, problem solving for survival—

Erik: But see, plants have this also, but it's a completely different web structure.

Me: So, the consciousness of animals is just more complex, not necessarily better?

Erik: There you go. I like that.

Me: How exactly are you able to communicate with animals? How specific can discussions get between you and animals?

Erik: They have these energy "thought bubbles" I can merge into or tap in to, but we don't have to stop with animals; plants have thought bubbles too. [Humans] just don't have the instruments to measure them and their activity. Now, there are a bunch of articles written about animals as spiritual beings—do they have beliefs? They do. They operate by the same morale system—

Jamie: "Morale," Erik?

Erik: Oh, "morals." They operate by the same system of morals.

Me: So, how exactly do you communicate with animals through telepathy?

Erik: If you can, imagine that there's an invisible translator sitting between you and the dog. You say something; it gets translated and then sent to the dog. It's that same sensation of when you know someone is staring at you. You know how you can feel their gaze, right? Then you turn to look, and you find it's true.

Me: Yeah, sure. Seems like we talked about this before, but yeah, that happens to me all the time when I'm driving. I can feel the driver in the car next to me at a stoplight, staring at me. I must look funny.

Erik: Again, it has to do with energy merging, and having an awareness of all the information in that energy field. I just don't think humans recognize that awareness anymore. That's the part of us that's going to be waking up. So, sitting with your dog, and sending thoughts and receiving feelings, is going to be a common thing.

Me: Good! So, our thoughts get translated, go to the animal, and what? How does that work?

Erik: It's communicating more with emotions. We might use words, and these get translated into feelings. Then the dog might use their bark, their expression, or their internal imagery, and it gets translated to us as an emotion. Some people can see and envision what the animal's emotions are explaining.

Me: If you're communicating with emotions, how specific can your discussions be?

Erik: Oh, very specific. You can talk about God and about death. They can talk about what the robber looked like when he broke into the house.

Me: Oh, wow!

Erik: Hell yeah, they can be very useful participants in life. So, I just don't know why people ignore them so much.

Me: Aw, that's a shame. What do animals say about humans? Oh, boy, that answer's not gonna be a pretty one, huh?

Erik: The animals completely see us as people who "run" the world. They do recognize that, but they see us more as individual machines rather than emotionally connected. They're more connected to the collective consciousness, so they're one up on us.

Me: Oh, I bet. They seem more spiritual and can love so unconditionally.

Erik: Yeah, because their structures are different, Mom. They don't have the demands and stresses that we, as humans, have created for ourselves. I mean, we humans create hardships for animals, but animals don't create hardships for themselves, that's for sure. We've totally created this rat race. We can walk away from it too, but people are too afraid to totally move off the grid or move to a different country—or basically, to make any radical change. People feel like they can't survive because that's the way they've been programmed.

Me: Is there anything else that animals would like us to know?

Erik: Animals have a way of absorbing your negative energy. If your pet is sick, you need to immediately point a finger to yourself.

Me: Oh, I can see that. I can.

Erik: And Mom, animals can see untethered souls, guides, and stuff; and they see three dimensionally just like the way they see spirits, because animals are so open. They don't have a brain that works the way ours does. They don't have that part of the brain that can be negative, pessimistic, or analytical. They can't be self-critical.

Me: Yeah, sucks to be human sometimes.

Erik: They don't get worried, depressed, and—

Me: Because they're not here to endure the human experience—to evolve spiritually—like we are?

Erik: Right. They're not here to work through issues. So the part of the brain that derails humans so much—animals don't have. And they're not raised in religions that dismiss or criticize spiritual stuff. It's kind of the same as with small children! They haven't had a rigid belief system indoctrinated into them yet. Little kids can communicate with animals and spiritual beings telepathically too.

Me: I didn't know that!

Erik: And animals can visit you in dreams while you're asleep, by merging or moving their electrical energy into your field of consciousness. Sometimes you get more visual input from spiritual beings at night, when you're sleeping, than when you're awake.

Me: Very cool! A lot of blog members want to know why there is such horrendous animal suffering and cruelty. What's the purpose of this? Why do they have to endure such pain?

Erik: Well, there are various reasons for animals to return to the earthly plane, Mom. First of all, some go there to be our family members, as pets—

Me: I'm not crazy about calling them "pets." I like "family member" or "animal companion."

Erik (in mock irritation at my interruption): Ahem.

Erik: Those chosen to be with us as animal companions are assigned to us. Their souls are assigned to us just like guardian angel souls are.

Me: How cool!

Erik: So, they will sometimes come to us two, three, four times in one lifetime, in different animal bodies. They die, come here to Heaven, and wait and wait and wait for us to adopt the body of another animal. And then their soul goes into that body. A lot of the animals we interact with on the earthly plane are those we've known in many, many past lifetimes. Sometimes they're a falcon or a horse, or maybe an alligator or a big snake, or a dog or a cat. They can come as any form of any animal. A dolphin.

Me: That's so amazing, Erik!

Erik: They're trusting that we are going to treat them well, but they understand that that may not happen. Oh, and sometimes animal spirits come to people they know are going to be abusive to them, just like we choose to have relationships with human beings who we know might be abusive to us—to learn from that.

Me: Why? Why do animals choose that?

Erik: Well, the animal doesn't make that kinda choice to learn anything. Humans make these choices to either learn, teach, or both. Animals choose to be with humans who abuse them to teach, to nurture, to love, to support, to encourage, or just to make us laugh.

Me: So, we know about animal companion souls, but what about animals who are going to be used for food or made into fur coats or whatever? And what about animals who live in the wild?

Erik: The animals who live in the wild choose to come back to the earthly plane purely to enjoy their time there. Nothing to learn, nothing to teach each other; just to enjoy.

Me: And the animals we use for meat or clothing?

Erik: Those particular souls go to the earthly planes [for this purpose], and, before they're slaughtered, their souls pop out of the body and come back to the Heavenly plane. They leave their bodies really easily 'cause they don't design their deaths as something to experience. Sometimes we want to experience a painful death, but they never do that.

Me: Oh, that's a relief.

Erik: Sometimes animal souls will migrate to the earthly plane to be of service to human beings.

Me: By some sort of mutual agreement?

Erik: Yes.

Me: But why don't we treat them with more respect? Is it because we're just not evolved enough yet?

Erik: Yes, Mom. On the earthly plane, some people are still abusing their own children! On the earthly plane, you're always going to have people who are numbnuts.

[Jamie and I laugh.]

Jamie: That paints a different picture.

Erik: Well, I thought you'd like a refreshing change from "asshole."

[We all laugh.]

Erik: A lot of humans are very arrogant; they see human life as superior to other forms of life. But you're also always gonna have people who respect life, whether it's an animal or a plant or a bug or another human being; they respect life. Now, when people encroach on an animal's property, it might hurt the human; a wasp might sting you, an alligator might bite or eat you. But it's not a disrespect thing; it's a survival thing. When there are animal abuses beyond the simple slaughtering of them for their meat or their fur, like using them in cruel lab testing or other acts that cause mass suffering—

Me: Yeah?

Erik: That's almost always for raising conscious awareness—to teach humankind about mutual respect, humility, and unconditional love.

This is usually a joint effort between human and animal spirits. They work together to manifest these atrocities as learning experiences for the collective consciousness.

Me (teasingly): Atrocities? Pretty big word for a little boy!

Erik: Hey, my vocabulary is getting better. Once I cut out most of the curse words, I had to find something else to fill the void.

Me: Wow, you must have a huge grasp of the English language, then!

[Erik and I both laugh.]

Erik: The large human ego, [and] the lack of connection [to] and respect [for] all living things—these are behind so much cruelty to animals, and all living creatures, really. Let's get really technical. Plants are living. Take a moment and think about the trees in the Amazon.

Me: Yeah.

Jamie: Oh, he's pretty rowdy right now!

Erik (sadly): Mom, you should see the emotions—oh!

Me: How terrible.

Jamie: Oh, that just made my stomach turn.

Erik: You should see the emotion when the trees are getting cut and mowed down and burned. There are levels of screams that you guys don't hear.

Me: Oh, I'm sure.

Erik: All that comes from that place [(the Amazon)].

Me: How awful, Erik. There are times I'm ashamed to be human. And it's all in the name of having exotic furniture and stuff.

Erik: Yeah, and land—pasture for cows. It needs to be stopped. [At the same time], what many people call God is not a judging god. We only judge ourselves. And so, if that doesn't feel right to you, like eating an animal or cutting down trees, you should never do it; never cross your own judgment.

Me: Okay, so basically, if it doesn't feel right for you, then don't do it.

Erik: Right, that's how God works through us.

Me: Is there some sort of spiritual contract between animals and us when we eat them?

Erik: It's a life cycle. It's not that it shouldn't be done, but it does need to be done with awareness. It shouldn't be done in mass factories. It's all about respect and compassion for all living things.

Me: I love these types of questions. What happens when animals hibernate? What happens to their spirits? Or plants—what happens to their spirits when they die back in the winter before they return in the spring? Do they go out traveling all over the planet or the universe, like taking a little break or vacation?

Erik: Well, the dying back of plants, and animals going into hibernation—those are the same thing. They pull deep within themselves for a moment of rest. Plants pull into their roots or the core of the stalk, but the soul doesn't leave the plant or animal when they do that. It's more like an extended dream state.

After listening to the insights Erik has imparted, my perspective has expanded. Knowing that there is no hierarchy among all life forces and knowing that even inanimate objects have some form of consciousness makes me feel connected—connected to my surroundings and connected to life. Understanding the nature of consciousness also gives me a broader perspective about myself. I am more than my body and brain, but all of these are intricately woven and define who we are.

11

TIME AND SPACE

Here, Erik guides us on a safari through the nature of both time and space. What he shares is uncannily aligned with the findings from world-renowned physicists from all corners of the Earth. At times, I struggled with these concepts, probably because it's difficult to describe nonlinear concepts using linear language. I highly recommend placing a bottle of Advil or Tylenol within your reach as we embark on this mind-bending yet illuminating journey.

How Time Works . . . It's About Time

Me: How does time work over there, Erik?

Erik: It doesn't. There is no such thing. The only way I'm reminded about time is—Well, I'm reminded every day when I'm with you guys there on the earthly plane. Time, because there is no hunger or need for sleep, is more like an ongoing circle instead of a linear thread of time where you go, "Oh, I'm hungry, it's lunchtime," or "Oh, I'm hungry, it's dinnertime," or "Oh, I'm tired, it must be bedtime." I guess it's the construct or constraints we have to have in order to be able to deal with things like that on the earthly plane. Time helps us conceptualize changes in state, sequences, cause and effects, and other time-related things that are a necessary part of the human experience.

[So proud of my little genius!]

Me: Well, how do *you* perceive time, and how does that dovetail into our concept of time, our construct? How does it reconcile with past and future lives?

Jamie: He pulls out—it looks like a Slinky—and he's stretching it and collapsing it, and stretching it and collapsing it—like a big spring.

Me: Cool!!

[Long pause as Jamie listens]

Jamie (giggling): He's just rattling off all kinds of things! Now, Erik, slooooow dooown! Talk really slowly for this, because it boggles my mind.

Erik: All right. When—

[Pause]

Jamie: Simple, Erik! More simple!

[Pause]

Jamie (chuckling): He's just laughing at me! No, no, no, Erik. Simpler will be easier to write about, and then you can get more complicated as we go.

Me: Yes, please. Dumb it down for us.

Erik: Within each dimension, there are different measurements of time. Let's start there.

Me: Okay.

Erik: When we're human, time for us is taught in a linear pattern. Let's take language. It's through the very linear human language that sequences are possible. It allows us to arrange events and actions sequentially. With that sequential language, present moments become surrounded by past moments and future moments. So, it's a human fabrication. Think about all the tenses we use: past, present, and future.

Jamie: What is that, Erik? He's saying "A to B, *tick, tock, tick, tock*," and he does his hand like a clock.

Erik: You humans don't go backward. You only go forward and only at a certain speed. Now, in the dimension we reside [in] as humans, there is a measurement that's not applied, and it happens to all of us—where time speeds up and slows down. It's like a breath: you can breathe in deep and hold it and slow down your heart rate; or you can breathe quickly and bring up your heart rate. This happens, say, when we get in a car and we know we're running late, but we don't speed and we still get there on time—maybe even a little early. And then we wonder how that happened!

Me: Ah!

Erik: Because you hit the red lights like you always do, you stopped at the traffic signs, you let people in front of you, and you still made it on time.

Me: Uh-huh. That has happened to me many times.

Erik: And there are those who think they have plenty of time. They gather their items together, which should take just a minute, but ten minutes is gone. Time speeds up.

Me: Or like when you're working on a project and you're really "in the zone," completely immersed in it, then you look at the clock, and what seemed like an hour ends up being three.

Erik: Yes. "In the zone." That's what we're going to talk about, because that's an emotional state of being.

Jamie: And he's pointing his finger like, "I'm talking about a point."

Me: Oh, so we better pay attention!

Jamie (giggling): His finger is just going to town.

Erik: It's an emotional state of being. With joy—not happiness—what do you think time does, speed up or slow down?

Me: Slow down? Oh, heck, I don't know. It probably depends on what side of time you're on. It depends on your point of reference. I'm so confused!

Erik: That's true. Most of the time, with joy, there's expansion. And in that expansion, time feels elusive—but it speeds up.

Me: Oh, it speeds up! Once you get out of it, you see that time has sped up. While you're in it, it seems to be—

Erik: Expansive, huge.

Me: And then after it's over, you think, "Wow, where did the time go?"

Erik: Yeah, think of your wedding, Mom: you're getting married, you're walking down the aisle—everything just seems larger than life. And then when the night's over, you feel like you only had thirty minutes.

Me: Yeah. Okay.

Erik: Now think about grief—the grief state of mind.

Me: Oh, boy. Time goes on forever.

Erik: Forever. It's really narrow-minded. It's like looking straight down, only at your feet. And time moves very slowly.

Me: So, is this the Slinky? Are you saying that if you're an ant crawling on the Slinky while it's stretched out, it seems like the distance you travel from one end to the other is longer; but since the Slinky hasn't actually grown in length, it's really not longer? And the opposite occurs when the ant is crawling on the Slinky when it's compressed?

Erik: Yes! That's how our emotional state of being affects time—the human construct of time. So language sort of frames it, and emotions can expand or contract it.

Me: Fascinating.

Erik: Mom, don't you notice how, when people grieve or they have hardships or challenges, they age so fast?

Me: Yes, because I've aged ten years in the past year. And look at all the presidents and how they get so gray so quickly.

Erik: But when people are joyful, their bodies stay youthful.

Me: Yeah.

Erik: That's time. That's a measurement of time.

Me: Wow, interesting!

Erik: So, on the earthly dimension, time is a function of language, motion, and emotion. Motion and language create your perception of time, and emotion expands or contracts it. Time exists only in consciousness. Outside of consciousness, it doesn't [exist].

Me: Whoa. That's a mind-bender, Erik!

Erik: Now, when you go beyond the dimension you live in—uh, okay, on Earth, you find that time can have different measurements. It can have—bear with me—a front side and a back side. The front side can be what you're focused on. You focus on it; you create it. You focus on expansion—you can do that. The back side is when there's no focus, where there's no measurement. Time can be as it is. This is when everything happens at once.

Jamie: Oh! I'm arguing with him just a little bit, because he says that in the truth of realities that we can understand, time is all happening at once. There's no future, there's no past. There just "is," and that's basically how time is for them over there in Erik's dimension.

Me: Okay.

Jamie: So, my question to him was, "Are you really trying to tell me that something grander, like the cycle of Earth, is being created, lived on, and destroyed all at the same time?'"

[Pause]

Jamie: He looks at me and laughs and goes, "Yep."

Me: So, we are living our past and future lives at the same time we live our present lives, I suppose?

Erik: Yes, yes!

Me: Okay. So, when people over there reincarnate, are they still there in Heaven, living that new life?

Erik: Yes, yes, Mom. Exactly.

Me: This is so interesting. So what is time shaped like over there? Is it just a point? Is it a web, a loop? I'm talking about the whole, grand scale of past, present, and future.

Erik: I get what you're saying. If you need a visual, take the web, put some waves in it, and make every line intersect. So, you can travel to *any* location you want: any dimension or any future or past or present point. It's all a moment point. It's all happening at once.

Me: Okay. And what are those intersections?

Erik: Lives. Intersections of lives. We have to speak in terms of past lives because, as humans, time is linear, and you don't believe in the future until you've walked in it. So we don't even talk about future lives; that sounds like science fiction. But soon, the term "future life" will be just as common as the term "past life." What do you think Leonardo da Vinci was tapping into?

Me: Oh, yeah!

Erik: You look at his sketches and designs, and you can see how he was clearly traveling across time and dimensions, and then logging what he was experiencing.

Jamie (in mock frustration, like a strict schoolteacher fussing at an unruly student): Erik! *ERIK!* Slow down!

Erik: You can also look at past, present, and future lives this way. Think of a wagon wheel. Your soul is the hub and each life you're living is a spoke. The lives retract back to the hub when you die—when that piece of you is reabsorbed—and it extends down the spoke as you are born and live your life. And the wheel is rolling in the mud creating a track. That track is your perception of time. All your lives are happening at the same time, but to you, they seem to progress linearly.

Me: That's so cool, Erik. You're so great at simplifying things with analogies. I have a couple more questions about the concept of time. You know, it seems like when we ask one question, three or four more come up. Here are a few: Does time exist solely as a function of motion? Is it created by motion? So, if everything in the universe were stopped and then started again, there'd be no way to determine just how long it had been stopped, right? In other words, does time exist only as a function of moving energy?

Erik: Yes.

Me: Anything more on that?

Erik: No, just that [time is] a human construct that's created by movement through a string of creations. One moment is created, then another, then another; and the consciousness—the energy that is consciousness—moves from one creation moment point to the next. That's how the time illusion is created.

Me: So, when you look at us, do we look like we're going in slow motion, or do we seem to be frozen in time? And when we see you, do you seem to be moving faster? I'm just trying to get an understanding of the perspective from both sides of the veil.

Erik: When we communicate with humans, we move in their plane, their realm.

Me: Okay.

Erik: Yes, we can move at the speed of light, so we can be at the front door, and then you turn around and we can be at the back door.

Me: Okay. Wow. So when you look at us, do we look like we're moving really, really sllllowwwwly since you move faster?

Erik: We can look at you like that.

Jamie: He's laughing!

Erik: It's not a preference, usually, 'cause it ain't pretty.

Me: Oh, God, I bet not!

Erik: But sports are fun to watch that way. We don't need a slow-mo camera.

Me (chuckling): Well, yeah, right. So you can see us just like you would have when you were alive?

Erik: Yes, the same. We can see you however we want—at whatever speed we want—but we usually prefer the earthly time speed.

Me: Okay, Erik, you say you're learning—you learn new things—but that's kind of a linear action, right? First you don't know information A, and then you do.

Erik: Yeah.

Me: So, how does that jive in a place with no time?

Erik: It's like when you take the time to merge with something that you have experienced before. That's when you comprehend. That's when you learn about it. So it's not like sitting down with a book, turning one page after another.

Me: But if you learn, that means you didn't know something before, and if you have a "before" and an "after," that means there's a time sequence there.

Erik: Well, don't take the idea of learning as having a new experience. If you imagine—

Jamie (chuckling at what he's saying): Clever!

Erik: —stacking a bunch of plates, so the top plate is the one you see the most. It's the one you interact with; it's the one you use the most. But learning, for us, means we already know all the plates, but we're taking the plate from the bottom and putting it on the top. So, you can tap in to what you want to know, bring it to the surface, and it eventually becomes the second plate in the stack instead of the first. Then it moves to the third place, on down the line. The simplicity comes from focusing on the top plate of remembered information.

Me: Oh, brilliant!

Erik: We're just bringing that information closer. Remembering. Bringing it closer to the surface.

Me: That is such an awesome way to explain it!

Erik: Yeah, so in a way, you can see time as a vertical stack of plates, all standing on one point, instead of a horizontal line of plates where you jump from one to the next, past to present to future. With the vertical stack of plates, you don't have to move in a linear sequence of time; but with the horizontal stack, you do.

Me: Okay, here's another question I was thinking about. It must be very challenging for you, Erik, to communicate with, interact with, and observe us when we are linear and you are not; how do you do that?

Erik: It's actually not that confusing!

Me: Oh, I'm confused just asking the question!

Erik: It's like having a pet turtle.

[Jamie and I laugh hard. Erik and his metaphors!]

Erik: You put it down, and you can run and do, like, a thousand errands—get in your car, go away and look at other things, go watch a movie, and then come back, and your turtle has just moved a little bit.

Me (giggling): Oh no! We're your pet turtles!

Erik: That's kind of how it is to view humans on a linear path.

Jamie (laughing hard): That's brilliant, Erik!

Me: Yeah, that's really good! I like that! Erik, you're so smart, sweetie. Be sure to clean our cage, though. When I was little, I had a tiny pet turtle, and sometimes I'd forget to clean its bowl, and it wasn't pretty! I'd hate to think that that's going to be the first pet that greets me when I cross over—this slimy green thing with algae and horrible, grungy, pond scum hanging all over it, saying, "Why didn't you clean my bowl?"

[Erik laughs.]

Me: What about space? Is there space where you are? What is space, really? Not outer space, you know, but—

Erik (laughing): There's definitely space. We have outer space; we have space—

Me: So, of course, space does exist. Is space the canvas we paint our realities on, or . . .

Erik: It continues endlessly.

Me: Oh, yeah. Infinite.

[Long pause]

Me: Anything else?

Jamie (chuckling): He's giving me a visual. I don't even know how to describe it! It's like a square box—a glass box. It's very small, and it's sitting on a shelf in a room with a whole bunch of other little glass boxes. When you get close to the box, there's a light in it.

Erik: We've trained ourselves to think we can fit our existence and what we know in a box—that we have parameters and boundaries. So, when people talk about space and the "space-time continuum," it shatters their glass box, and it's very uncomfortable for people to do this.

Me: Yeah, I bet.

Erik: And so, people would rather say, "Ah, I don't need to know that here." You know what? They're right. That's why we come to Earth. We come to narrow down; we come to simplify; we come to gain that "glass box" image. So, if you want to talk about the nature of space, I think we really need to sit down and ask, "What do you want to present? What are you trying to show?" I think the best lesson is this: It's great to be narrow-minded while we can, because life is short. Of course you can ponder the infinite nature of space and a more expansive perspective, but you can't live life from that perspective if it means not completing your spiritual contracts and the lessons you're supposed to learn on the earthly plane. You have to live life from the perspective of a human being. Let me back up. You have to live life as a spiritual being living a human experience and not like a "free as a bird" eternal spirit. You won't learn jack shit like that.

Me: Yeah, we need to concentrate on the lessons we're here to learn by using the duality of the earthly playing field to our best advantage. It's too hard to create that duality—that contrast—when we have the expansive perspective as an untethered soul, our infinite realities and probabilities and dimensions and selves.

Jamie: He's putting his finger up in the air.

Erik: You're right! We do have to concentrate on a narrower perspective when we're in the physical, and what's the most important thing to concentrate on over there? Honor. That is a concept of love.

Me: Ah!

Erik: Open communication from one human being to another.

Me: Yep.

Erik: And that means love for a plant, a tree, an insect, an animal, any living being.

Me: Love for life, period. I mean, there are all sorts of love. Now, when we're on this little stage, doing this little school play called the human experience, what you're saying is that we need to concentrate on the play itself and the roles we have in it. We have to narrow things down and focus on the task at hand?

Erik: Yep. That's the simple glory in life.

Me: Okay, so, back to what "space" is like where you are? I know it's not entirely the same as the space we live in here in the 3-D realm, but . . .

Erik: Well, there is that too. It's some of both, and I know that's hard to understand. So much of it is made of light and energy, but there is a 3-D aspect to it too. We have homes here, as you know, plus there's beauty and nature and stuff. It's like love, and love has an energy of its own. You feel like someone would feel in outer space. There's no gravity, so there's a feeling of pure lightness—no heaviness at all. And when you look at angels, you can look right through them. It's just light, all light.

[This next question seemed a bit off-topic, but eventually, it had to do with the nature of time.]

Me: Wow, okay. Let's see, here's one I've asked you before through another route, Erik, but so many people have this question. So, how come we sometimes get different answers to the same question through different spirit communicators and translators, or even different answers to the same question from the same one?

Jamie: Different answers to the same question from the same spirit translator?

Me: You know, like, say you ask what your destiny is or what your last life was like. You can get different answers from different spirit translators, and sometimes different answers from the same translator in two different sessions.

Erik: You have to remember that we're not fixed, Mom. Humans like to see that they're fixed because they're focused on the linear. But no, we're always changing. Your own free will—or the free will of a stranger two thousand miles away—can bump you in a new direction.

Me: So, we can change the future. Can we change the past too?

Erik: Yep. And every time you ask a different spiritual communicator, or even when you go to the same one, it's a different moment.

Me: Oh, okay!

Erik: So the answers have variables, even though, on Earth, humans want to believe the answers are solid or fixed.

Me: Okay.

Erik: And sometimes you can go to any communicator anywhere and get the same answer!

Me: Uh-huh, because your intent is focused on that probable past or future.

Erik: Exactly. And since all spirit translators are humans and humans have filters created by their analytical mind, sometimes they're going to be wrong.

Me: And Jamie has zero filters.

Erik: Just about! Plus, she lets me cuss and be who I am. I love that about her.

What did I take away from Erik's insights on time and space? We humans create constructs for both in order to get the most out of our experience on Earth. We have to focus our perspectives on each sentence, on each page of the book of life, rather than focus on the infinite number of volumes sitting on our bookshelf.

12

MATTER AND REALITY

As we venture further in our exploration of the mysteries that define life and our existence, we delve into the nature of reality itself. One could say that this waypoint is indeed the Holy Grail in our quest; because matter to which we are accustomed in our 3-D reality is nothing more than frozen light, and reality is everything—all-inclusive yet elegantly simple.

All About Matter

Me: I've been reading a lot about how matter is created, how reality is created, and there are a couple of theories I've been reading about. One is the Wave Structure of Matter Theory, which has to do with interacting spherical waves; and the other is the Vortex Theory, which claims that electrons, protons, and neutrons are holes in space, and vortices connect them in 3-D and 4-D space. Argh! It's so complicated for me to grasp. So, is there any truth to these two theories?

Jamie: When you talk about the vortex, [Erik] puts his lips together like he's going to whistle, but he only makes a blowing sound.

Me: Okay.

Erik: That's just to blow wind up your skirt.

[Jamie and I laugh.]

Erik: It's a brilliant idea, but it can never be proven.

Me: Oh, really?

Erik: Yeah, and you'll see that in the next five or six years, science will be able to identify a lot of what we're experiencing. The Wave Structure of Matter [Theory] has more validity, but no theory out there captures the total picture accurately.

Me: Yeah.

Erik: I have a thought: I think it's so wild that because people "play" science, or because they make things or put them together, they think they created it!

Me: Yeah!

Erik (with mock importance and pomposity): MAN, THE CRE-ATOR! The more I sit and look at that MAN, THE CREATOR, it just blows my mind—because I [once] thought: "I can destroy that, and I can create this," but it's absolutely not true. It's a falsity, worse than wearing rose-colored glasses. Humans think they're the center of creation in a way, but energy can neither be created nor destroyed, remember?

Me: Yeah, Physics 101. So really it's our perceptions that create and destroy.

Erik: You can destroy and create your perceptions too.

Me: Ah!

Erik: The only power you have, as humans, is to manipulate, to move, to shape.

Me: And our consciousness, our thoughts, and our free will do that?

Erik: Yes. Our intention toward something manipulates it. It doesn't really create or destroy it; it just shapes it. Reality shapes our intentions, and our intentions shape our perception of that reality; it's a back-and-forth thing. There's a communication between nature and human, reality and human.

Me: Oh!

Erik: Just think about it, Mom: When you take a walk in a forest, and you look up and you see these magnificent trees, it takes your breath away. Just that sight, that smell, that feeling, that experience changes you. It changes the way you respect the place: It changes how you tell others about it. In the same throw, that awe, that experience that you have—the trees, the plants, the ground—the Earth feels it and absorbs it. Our plants and our nature are the best recyclers of energy. Just think of all the negativity and all the wars that are out there; and pollution—how well do you think nature is recycling it now?

Me (somberly): Yeah, what a shame. One reader asks these questions: "So, the nature of reality is basically like waves? Do they turn off and on in a particular sequence? Is reality like a river that flows and bends, twisting and turning as it follows the contours of the banks? Do the energetic waves respond to input?" We know the waves respond to input—that our thoughts, our intention, and our attention manipulate them, right?

Erik: Right.

Me: So, what is that "thing" that we're manipulating?

Erik: Waves. Energy waves. Energetic vibrations. High-frequency waves, low-frequency waves—this is what we shape like the clay a sculptor molds into a statue. It's our food. It can affect the growth, the life, the air. It can affect the emotions of a person. A thought, our mere internal thinking—the most simple thing we do—creates a change and manipulates the energy vibrations around us.

Me: Fascinating!

Erik: The only thing that binds us is our belief system.

Me: Yeah, our perceptions.

Erik: Exactly. Perceptions. We're taught the perception that the table is solid. You put the glass down; the glass will stop upon the table. That's a fixed concept within humans, and it's very hard for a parent not to teach a child these things.

Me: Oh, God, yeah! And the collective consciousness molds these perceptions and belief systems too, probably.

Erik: Yes!

Me: So, we know that thought creates reality, and [the process is] immediate in your dimension. Thought manifests things instantaneously.

Erik: Uh-huh.

Me: Do you have to sit there and concentrate constantly to keep maintaining a manifestation like a house or a meadow with purple grass? How can the house, for instance, stay real for so long? It would be exhausting to constantly think "a house, a house, a house" to maintain its existence. Do you have to do that for it to remain manifested?

Erik: So, looking at it the opposite way: if I stop thinking about the house, will the house stop being in existence? Is that what you mean?

Me: Yes. That's exactly what I'm asking. That takes an awful lot of concentration.

Erik: No, you'd think it would, because it's so much harder to manifest there on the earthly plane. So you think it would take a lot of sit-down time, drawing time, but it's not like that. As long as we are using [the house] and thinking about it, it remains in existence.

Me: Okay.

Erik: But if we're not thinking about it or using it—if no one is thinking about it or using it, it is not needed and it's not in existence. Then, as soon as it's recalled again, it's there. It reappears. When it's not in existence, it's not destroyed; it just doesn't take up space. Thought creates reality through energy. One plus one equals two. So you have thoughts plus energy making a new reality.

Me: Can you explain more?

Erik: Thoughts are projections of your electrical energy, so when you're thinking, you are also communicating. You're building your store of electrical energy and determining how much of it you can move through your body.

[I gather that he means thoughts, projected as intentions, are forms of energy that create matter and therefore reality, in accordance with Einstein's $E=mc^2$.]

Me: Okay, say I'm walking down a path. This is an illusion, right? Am I constantly manifesting the path in front of me as a go? Am I constantly, instantly manifesting each moment that I take a step?

[Long pause]

Jamie (giggling): He's doing that whole "rub the chin and think" pose.

Me: Okay, let's say there's a mile-long path, but I don't see the last half of the mile in the distance, because I really haven't created it for myself. Does that last half mile then not exist until I create it during future steps in subsequent moments? Am I constantly updating the length of that path as I go?

Erik: Yeah, you're constantly updating the path, but if you're sharing space with others who have the same vision—they're on that same mile-long walk. Like maybe there's somebody fifteen feet in front of you, and that's something they've been creating. Since you're both in the same dimension, you can see what they've created. So it's a universal—a unity point. It's not just an individual light beam.

Me: How do you create realities together with other souls? There must be some sort of cooperation, then—to have many souls living in the same thought-created environment, for example.

Erik: We agree to cooperate telepathically, but there's a caveat. You can turn into reality only that which dovetails with your destiny. If it doesn't agree with your destiny, you can't create it.

Me: I can't imagine that people would want to create something that's not part of their destiny.

Erik: Oh, a lot of people do!

Me: Well, why wouldn't it work? Why can't you create your reality regardless of your destiny?

Erik: When we come to the earthly plane, we have a spiritual blueprint. Our thoughts and our actions must work toward accomplishing what's on that spiritual blueprint. If we finish that, we can accomplish more. Say, for example, a woman is married to a rich dude and she's miserable and wants out, but she knows she has to work full-time if she divorces him. She might think, "I don't want to. Can't I just win the lottery?" That's not going to happen, because no matter how much time, energy, and passion she puts toward winning the lottery, she won't; because it would derail her spiritual forward movement, which includes developing independence and empowerment by getting a full-time job and letting go of Mr. Sugar Daddy.

Me: Okay, I get it. But surely the rules of the game are different in the afterlife. What about people who are on the other side—like you, Erik? You can pretty much create whatever reality you want, right?

Erik: Yep, no caveat there.

Me: Pretty handy. Okay, so what is dark matter?

Jamie: He's clarifying—is it dark matter or gray matter you're talking about?

Me: No, dark matter. You know, like there's dark energy and there's dark matter. It's a physics thing.

Jamie: Well, he's telling me he's trying to figure out in what context you are wanting the answer, because you can look at dark matter as being an entity—as in a spirit—or dark matter in the case of not an entity.

Me: Not an entity; like something in the universe—something that makes up a large portion of the universe as we know it.

Erik: It's a compacted force, almost like a vacuum field.

Jamie: The way he's showing it is there's so much energy in the universe that it appears to be empty or dark.

Me: Uh-huh.

[I'm floored by how closely this idea of the infinitely dense vacuum aligns with physicist Nassim Haramein's unified field theory, something I learned about months after this session.[4]]

Jamie (to Erik): What do you mean? Like pound per— The density of it, yeah. Heavy, heavy density.

[Long pause]

Erik: It's like a magnetic force. It's attracted to itself, and so it kind of breeds. It pulls things in—sucks them in and holds them down.

Me: Okay, I read somewhere that there really is no "God particle," and we need to stop trying to find the smallest unit. Instead, we need to see that there is a pattern of infinite division—infinitely large and infinitely small. Most of reality is space. Matter doesn't define space; space defines matter. Is that true?

Erik: Absolutely. Right on.

Me: You know, they say that all the universes are different membranes shaped as sheets and donuts and cylinders—and so on—and that maybe sometimes these membranes collide and the points of collision create matter. Is that something that's possible?

Jamie (laughing hard): Erik's laughing.

Erik: Absolutely possible, Mom, but knowing how things are built is not going to give you more understanding about what you're in.

Me: Oh, yeah, I know. But I just find this stuff interesting.

Erik: Why are people trying to focus all their energy on unraveling mysteries like that instead of understanding why they're in it? We gotta look at that.

Me: Oh, all right, then. So you want me to leave all that to the physicists?

Erik: Yeah, perfect.

Me: Okay, here's another one: Does nonsentient—you know, non-thinking consciousness, including electrons—create matter or reality also? I mean, it is a consciousness after all, even if it's an unaware consciousness.

Erik: I pose my first question! What makes you think it's not a conscious, thinking—

Me: Well, maybe it is—I don't know! Can electrons think, then?

Erik: Sad thing is, we try to make everything think like we do.

Me (chuckling): Oh, dang, can't we human beings get anything right?

Erik: Try again. [Electrons] do think; they comprehend; they have actions and reactions, and—

Me: Well, are they self-aware, or are they more like how you describe rocks—beings with "a primitive, unaware consciousness"?

Erik: They're self-aware only when they're around something else, but not in a way you think. It's hard for me to explain it in a way you'll understand.

Me: Is that why entanglement works?

Jamie: I haven't read anything about that. What is it?

Me: Once two electrons interact, then they'll continue to influence each other, even if they're light-years away. At least that's how I understand it.

Jamie (surprised): Really?

Me: Yeah, I think Einstein called it "spooky action at a distance."[5] He didn't completely understand why they behaved that way. So, can they problem-solve?

Erik: Yes.

Me: Really? But can they create matter just like we can with our thoughts? Can electrons and other particles create their own reality?

Erik: Uh, they can consciously problem-solve, so if they solve a problem, then yes, they are creating matter. But to think of it as, you know, matter that you can touch with your hand—

Me: Uh-huh.

Erik: It's not matter like that, Mom, and their problem-solving ability is not the same as with human beings.

Me: Wow. I bet that'd be hard to explain to me further too!

Erik: Yeah, 'cause you don't really have the language for it.

Me: Okay, let's say there's a glass sitting on top of a table and it's seen by three observers. Does each observer create his or her own 3-D space with an entirely different glass? Does each sentient and each non-sentient consciousness, including the atoms or electrons of the table, the chairs, and so on, create this too—so that the reality of the glass really exists in multidimensional space, you know, in an infinite number of dimensions, made up of each space, of each consciousness, from each observer?

Jamie: He's laughing.

Me: Oh, God, I'm so confused. And so, is it defined as one glass on one table only by mutual agreement, because we communicate it as such to each other?

Erik: Okay, this might burst your bubble. The focus and the awareness have to be on the glass when it's made, like in a factory. Then it's actually created and brought into the three-dimensional plane. And just because a glass sits on a counter, a table, or in a cabinet behind closed doors, for that matter, it doesn't mean that it disappears, because it's already been created. So it doesn't take focus for it to exist.

Me: Oh, okay. So you don't have to keep thinking about something for it to persist.

Erik: Right. All you have to do is know it exists.

Me: Okay. Boy, that would take a lot more work than I'd be able to put out.

Erik: Now, step back and look at it this way: I think that's what whoever brought up the whole "glass on the table" thing wanted to focus on. He didn't want to focus on the small things like the curtains and walls and floors. He wanted to focus on the whole illusion of reality.

Me: Oh, I see.

Erik: Now, that right there takes everybody in the game to focus and co-create the reality you know as the earthly plane. And once you're in it, you do have some part of the control; and within that control we can create and destroy, move and change. We create a bench made out of concrete, we can destroy the bench made of concrete. But it doesn't take conscious-thought effort for that concrete bench to be real. We've already done that, because we believe in the whole formatted system. Do you get it?

Me: No, I'm so confused.

Erik: I don't know any other way to explain it. Everything has consciousness. That's why people heal with crystals and certain energy-carrying stones. Plants too. Everything on the Earth carries a consciousness. When you walk into a home, you can feel a unique energy, because the home sucks in the energy of everyone that has lived there. So homes even have a consciousness. Okay, so about electrons and atoms—yes, they can create matter, but it needs the soul of the human to assist it.

Me: So, these can create matter, but they need the consciousness of a soul to help?

Erik: Yeah.

Me: That's like the theory in physics that you need an observer—I guess that's consciousness in this case—to change a wave into a particle. That parallels with changing a thought into reality. Mass and Energy. $E=mc^2$. Wow. It's all coming together.

Erik: And each observer sees it differently. Remember, everything flows. Everything is energy, and it flows and slows down to create matter; and that matter flickers in and out of existence, like a ripple or a wave on top of the ocean. It's there, it's not there; it's always changing. The glass is never the same from one moment to the next.

Me: So, let me see if you've learned anything else about this question since I asked you a while back. What is our "true reality," here or where you are? Where are we alive and where are we dreaming?

Erik: There is no differentiation, Mom. You're alive on Earth; you're alive in the afterlife. Anywhere the soul travels—anywhere it is—it's alive and well. The soul can travel to different planets; it doesn't just have to travel to Earth. Hell, we can travel around the universe with aliens if we want.

Me: So, the "true reality" is—

Erik: Wherever the soul happens to be at the time. And when a soul is over here in the afterlife, that doesn't mean the earthly plane doesn't exist. It's still a reality of another dimension; it's just a perspective thing. Our "true reality" is wherever we happen to be at the time.

Me: But where's our true home, then?

[I just wanted to confirm what he said before.]

Erik: Here. We go to the earthly plane when we go on vacation.

Me: Damn, Erik. Some vacation! I want my money back! I need a new travel agent!

Erik: Guess what, Mom: you are your own travel agent! We are our own travel agents. We decide what we're going to experience!

Me: Well, that's it, then. I'm fired!

Erik (laughing): So no gifts on Boss's Day?

Me: No, not for me!

Erik (still laughing): I think many other people would feel that way, too!

The Nature of Death

Once I understood the process before and after death, I yearned to know more from a scientific standpoint—both the macro-view and the micro-view.

Me: Nassim Haramein, a physicist who helped to develop unified field theory, defines reality in a way that really makes sense to me. He said something that particularly sparked my interest—that there are black holes in atoms, and there are black holes in just about everything, from the infinitely small to the infinitely large. Meaning, we're essentially living in a black hole, and that's why everything we see in space is black. But if we were to go on the other side of the event horizon, we'd see this beautiful white light.[6] So, I'm just wondering if death is just a matter of crossing the event horizon from a black hole to a white hole.

Erik: I have firsthand experience here, Mom. It's exactly like that. You remain with the physical body for a time; it's like a time of adjustment. You don't get immediately "sucked up"—and that's exactly what it's like, a suction. But you can see. You can see. You're still on the Earth's plane, and you can see family and friends. You can look at your body, and then there's a sense of freedom. No gravity. It's a lightness that's difficult to explain. It's as if you get sucked up in this tunnel of bright light passing through the Earth's density. And you do come out on another side—the other side. It's beautiful. It's light.

Me: So I do think this guy's on to something. You cross an event horizon.

Erik: Yep, exactly. And it's what they say when you "cross over the veil." It's a very thin veil. It's just a thin veil that separates those sides, but it's dense, particularly toward the Earth.

The Physics of Death

Me: Energetically, what happens at the time of death? Does something happen to the wave pattern or the frequency of our energy? Does our energy pass into a white hole? What happens from a sort of physics perspective?

[Pause]

Jamie (to herself): From the physics perspective.

Erik: Well, um—

Me: In simple terms. You don't have to get elaborate, 'cause you might not even know, and we might not even understand it if you do. But what happens energetically at death?

Jamie: The visual that comes with it is [him] showing me a body that's just recently deceased, and the energy is separating from the matter.

Erik: The energy is separating from the matter it created.

Jamie: The way that I see it in my head is kind of on a cell level, and there are these sparks—it almost looks like when you rub your feet on the carpet, and then you tap someone and *zap!*

Me: Uh-huh. Okay. The sparks are on each cell? Coming from each cell?

Jamie: Yes. *Spuck, spuck, spuck, spuck.* So that the energy can escape the matter that it created, and this is how the matter is left behind. There's not like this spontaneous, mass exodus of, um, like—

Erik (to Jamie): What are you doing?

Jamie (to Erik): I have no idea! I'm just trying to watch! I don't know, but I feel extremely handicapped today when you're showing me images and talking!

Jamie (to me): What he's saying is . . . um, he's almost posing a question. If the energy leaves the body—if the soul leaves the body—why doesn't the body just completely disappear?

Me: Oh, my God! Yeah!

Jamie: Right? Because it was the energy of the soul—

Erik: Well, that's the difference! That's what I'm trying to tell you. There's this kind of spark—this kind of separation—and the energy that created the body, created the cells, created the muscles, created the bones, is leaving it behind. That's the whole idea of the death—[the creative energy] no longer wants the body that it put together and thrived in. That's why it becomes a shell.

Me: Ah, molting!

Erik: Because when it's alive, it's very much connected on every level. That's pretty much the first thing that takes place. Instant separation. *Pa-pa-pa-pa-pow!* I think here lies the answer of spontaneous combustion. It's those people whose energy couldn't leave its material makings behind, so it created sparks so violent and so strong that it actually— *POW!*—went into flames. These are people who have trouble letting go of everything. Even the body. After this, the energy collects; this is the soul energy. And when the soul energy is able to completely separate from the body, it's able to be identified as spirit. And it still uses the memories and the collection of characteristics that it created throughout that lifetime to journey itself back Home. So, if it believes in the tunnel—if it believes in the spirit, the demons or whatever—that's what it has to go through until it gets Home. It's self-powered until it arrives Home, and then it can be delivered a certain kind of truth.

Me: What do you mean by "delivered a certain kind of truth"?

Erik: It would be a truth that would match that spirit's understanding. In other words, when the soul arrives, it's still so connected to human understanding that we have to pose concepts in a certain way so that it can be understood. But then, once the spirit comprehends where it is and has a broader acceptance of knowledge, we can feed [it] deeper truths—broader truths and concepts that are larger than the body itself. That's why we keep saying that, when you die, you don't just get the keys to the city. You don't just instantaneously know everything, but that speed [of knowing] depends on your willingness. Your free will. In terms of earthly time, it takes some people years [while] it takes [other] people three minutes. So, there's no right or wrong here.

Me: When you say, "We can feed it deeper truths," who are "we"?

Erik: *We* are! I'm just trying to say, in general, the guides that show up and help. So, it'd be that person's personal guides or angels, or if there was a spiritual counselor who was dedicated to that person, that's who would show up. It might be deceased family members.

What Erik shared about the nature of death from an energetic, scientific standpoint was difficult for me to grasp initially. In a word, it was mind-bending, but I feel its truth. Plus, an explanation for the "myth" of spontaneous combustion was a bonus!

13

LOVE AND FEAR

Everything comes down to two root emotions: love and fear. This is the essence of the duality that defines the human experience and fuels our spiritual growth. Both have their crucial purposes. Both are inescapable. But in the end, we choose love over fear, because we *are* love, and we strive to become unconditional love. Now, let's explore these two polar emotions, with Erik as our guide.

The Nature of Fear

Me: Why is there fear, and how was that energy created? Where does it come from? Do we plan fear into our lives as part of our personality, so that when we come here, we can overcome it? Is it this environment on the planet that makes us fearful, or do we just develop it over time from the experiences we have here?

Erik: Fear developed through the environment, and it just *is*. All humans have fear of some kind; [it occurs] when we don't have a connection to love in a situation or with an issue. Fear is the absence of spiritual connection, meaning it's the relative absence of love, meaning it's the relative absence of light. It's part of that duality that's so important in the human experience. When we overcome fear, we rediscover love; we rediscover our spiritual divinity. And when we go

241

through that cycle of fear, overcoming fear, finding love over and over, in every issue that we gotta address. Well, that's the point of spiritual enlightenment, isn't it?

Me: Yeah, I guess peeling back the fear reveals the love and our connection with spirit, then?

Erik: Yep. And as humans, you wouldn't be able to see that connection with spirit without some component of fear. It's like you have to have the fear so you can peel back that layer, and *ta-da!* there's the love; there's my connection to spirit. Kinda like a magician whipping his hankie away and there's a vase of flowers.

Me: Yeah, I guess we have to put that extra step in there for the contrast, but sometimes duality really sucks.

Erik: I know. It can make life a crock of shit sometimes, but it's a really powerful tool.

Me: Wish we could just have some special truth goggles to see what we need to see. Be a helluva lot easier.

[Erik laughs.]

Erik: Fear comes from ego; it's not a soul-level thing. And there's a lot of reasons for humans to have fear: a fear of not being good enough, a fear of not being able to do something well. Fear helps to develop ego, and ego helps to develop fear. They go in a circle. Fear usually is an absence of connection to spirit—not complete absence, obviously, but a relative absence on a particular issue. But the point of ego is twofold: we need an element of ego to survive physically. Also, to get to love, sometimes our ego has to grow to the point that it destroys itself; that's how we reach rock bottom. Our ego spirals out of control, self-destructs, and leaves room for that inner space: conscious awareness—the real you. With all that ego shit out of the way, you clear the path toward love.

While I was communicating with Erik on my daily walk through the woods, he asked me to share an exercise for any or all of you to try.

Take a sheet of paper and divide it into two columns, one labeled *fear* and the other labeled *love*. In the *fear* column, list as many fear-based emotions as you can come up with:

abandonment	envy	paranoia
aggravation	false pride	pessimism
agitation	frustration	racism
anger	gluttony	rage
annoyance	greed	rejection
anxiety	grief	remorse
apathy	guilt	resentment
arrogance	impatience	resignation
competitiveness	indifference	revenge
condescension	insecurity	self-pity
confusion	intimidation	selfishness
contempt	jealousy	shame
denial	judgment	shyness
depression	lack of faith	stubbornness
despair	laziness	superiority
disappointment	loneliness	suspicion
discouragement	manipulation	uncaring
disgust	negativity	unwillingness
doubt	obsession	worry
dread	overwhelm	worthlessness
embarrassment	panic	

For me, grief belongs in both columns, because you have the fear of being without whatever you've lost, but you also have the love of what you've lost.

In the *love* column, list the emotions that you think are love-based:

acceptance	generosity	patience
arousal	gratitude	peacefulness
awe	grief	playfulness
beauty	happiness	positivity
calm	harmony	power
caring	honesty	pride (not false pride)
certainty	hope	relaxation
cheerfulness	humility	relief
comfort	humor	respect
compassion	inner strength	satisfaction
confidence	inspiration	self-love
contentment	interest	sharing
courage	joy	stability
determination	kindness	strength
empathy	longing	surprise
enthusiasm	loyalty	sympathy
faith	nurturance	trust
fascination	openness	understanding
forgiveness	optimism	unity

Erik wants you to make your own lists, of course. Then circle those fear-based words that most affect you, and think about all the various instances in your life, past or present, where they apply or have applied. If you want, you can think about those instances first, and then build the *love* and *fear* lists based on those.

Now, choose how you can replace your fear emotion with one from the *love* column. For instance, if you feel angry at someone who has hurt your feelings (this is Erik's example, by the way), then you can choose to project kindness to that person; you can choose to forgive him or her. I do this by envisioning myself sending pink light to that person's heart and watching in my mind's eye as their facial expression transforms from a scowl to a loving smile. It also helps to say this affirmation daily: "I have abundance in all things that honor my highest purpose." That pretty much covers it all: love, joy, opportunities, wealth, and so on. So remember, when you know you're grappling with a fear-based emotion, seek and replace it with a love-based one. When you're at a fork in the road, choose the path of love over the path of fear. It takes practice, but after all, that's what we're here for. We are meant to *become* unconditional love. Better yet, we're here to remember that we already *are* unconditional love.

14

THE NATURE OF HIGHER POWERS

The belief in a deity—or deities, plural—is an integral aspect of most of the world's religions. A while back, I asked Erik whether he had met such a being, and he said that as soon as he transitioned into the afterlife, he kept a low profile. He wanted to remain under the radar, because he was scared of being punished for having taken his own life. Once he realized there is no judgment or punishment on the other side, he promised me he would find out more. Because the existence of God (who we will refer to as "God" for the purposes of this conversation, as "God" is just one of many names for the concept of a higher power) is such an important part of many lives, I wanted to see whether Erik had done his homework as he'd promised. That said, God was on the top of my list of questions for this conversation. Jamie and I were surprised by Erik's discoveries.

Session about God

Me: So, tell me, Erik, have you had a chance to meet up with God yet?

Jamie: He's showing me this in my mind's eye. Erik called them "assemblies," where spiritual beings can attend talks or lectures given by God. Hmm, I've never seen that before. That's interesting.

Me: I guess He'd make a heck of a keynote speaker, huh?

Jamie: It's fascinating.

[Erik chuckles.]

Jamie: You're not teasing me, are you, Erik?

Erik (emphatically): NO! NO! This really does happen. I'm not kidding!

Me: So, how do you see God, Erik? Do you see God as a light? Do you see God as a being that has male or female energy?

Erik: As a light. As a bright, white, silvery light.

Me: How do you know it's God? To ask an interesting question, what makes you so sure that that's God?

Erik: Because when you're in spirit, there are things that you feel and know. You don't question everything like you do on the earthly plane, with your brain.

Me: Oh, okay!

Erik: We feel and know the truth.

Me: So, you have this knowingness?

Erik: Yes. I haven't gotten any personal audiences yet, but I have been exposed to God—not only the energy in Heaven. I've also been exposed to messages God shares that are meant for all of us as a whole. I believe that the spirits who find [them] it most insightful are the ones who are getting ready to come back to the earthly plane again.

Me: Interesting. Kind of like He sends messages through an "All Call" button on an intercom?

Erik: (chuckling) Yes, exactly.

Me: Now, does God have a male or female energy, Erik?

Erik: Androgynous. Both male and female, but you wouldn't call it one or the other.

[In a later session.]

Me: So have you met God personally yet, Erik? Or have you met God's true representation?

Erik: Well, we're all a true representation of God. So you're asking, have I met the pure Source of it?

Me: Uh-huh.

Erik: Absolutely. Wouldn't you want to do that too?

Me: Oh, yeah!

Erik: I mean, not everybody wants that; they don't get it. But yes, I wanted to sit down. I wanted answers.

Me (chuckling): Does He sit on a throne and have a long white beard?

[Jamie and I laugh.]

Erik: No, no throne. And again, there's no male or female with God.

Me: Okay.

Erik: But it's kind of like this feeling where you have all these questions, and you want these things to be resolved. You know, like, I went in there with all these things, these curiosities. Then as soon as I met God face to face, in front of— It was a light—an expansive light. Not much shape that I could describe—like the shape of a heart or of a person. I could tell It was much taller than me, though.

Me: Okay.

Erik: And as soon as I got into God's presence, I wanted to get closer and closer. All my emotions were turned inside out, and I welcomed it. I didn't wanna cover up anything; I didn't want to protect myself. I just wanted to walk closer to It, and then my list and everything I wanted to know just seemed so childish. It just seemed so irrelevant, because the closer you get to the Source, [the more] you know that This is [what matters]. And yet, when you walk away from It—when you separate yourself just a little bit—your questions come back. Mine did.

Me: Oh! Interesting!

Erik: And that's when you go, *Aw, why didn't I ask?* But then you remind yourself, *Well, I didn't need to know that, because when I was there, everything was in perfect accordance*, that life is playing out as life, and that there is this safety net that people don't wanna talk about—even all these negative things that are happening. It's all right. Everything is going to be just fine.

Me: Yep, I guess we all have happy endings after all is said and done. So, is that what we all yearn to do—go back to the Source eventually? That's the ultimate?

Erik: Yes, we talked about this before, and you can. You can completely surrender, merge yourself, but that's only done by your free will. If that's your goal of enlightenment, then that is what you will reach.

Me: But can you separate out again? I mean, once you go in there, once you—

[I realized after I asked this question that I had asked it before. Still, I hoped for confirmation and details.]

Erik: God will release you again. He did it once before. God's not controlling.

Me: So God is not a control freak, eh?

Jamie: Erik's cracking up.

Me: So, what is God made of and what is God, *really*?

Erik: I can't really answer that except to say it's like looking at the sun—just light. You can't even look without feeling total, total love, as if nothing else that happens affects you at all. This is the only explanation I could give you that you might understand.

Me: Yes, please dumb it down for me! But God has some sentient consciousness, right? Can the God Source communicate to you and you to It?

Erik: Oh, hell yeah, and it's very, very clear, Mom. The information comes like a wonderful pulsing of incredible energy that has a consciousness. You're just drawn to It, and the closer you get, the more you just feel love. I can't put it into words any more than that. God is energy. Energy is a living, thriving source that has divided and spread like some contagious—

Jamie (in mock frustration): He uses the word disease.

Me: Oh! Better watch out, Erik, lest God smite you—whatever that means.

Erik: You're placing judgment on a word, Mom. You're thinking that disease is a negative.

Me: Oh, yeah, that's right!

Erik: Disease can be extremely positive! It serves as a huge catalyst for a lot of people. But I just wanted to use the word "contagious," because that energy spreads everywhere! Without its existence, we wouldn't have created. We would not have created ourselves. I say that, because God is in all of us.

Me: Yeah, exactly.

Erik: There's such a stigma on the word "God." I really wish we could just erase that and come up with something else.

Me: Yeah, I guess it implies that It's a separate thing, and It's not.

Erik: You're right, It's not! So that question may well have been, "What am *I* made of?"

Me: Yeah, yeah. So you already told me some about when you spoke to God. Anything else?

Erik: Yeah.

Me: Okay, what about? Did you just shoot the breeze, like talk about the Super Bowl or say, "How 'bout them Yankees?"

Erik (chuckling): No, no. We all just sit on a red velvet couch and smoke cigars. That's what we do.

[Jamie and I laugh.]

Erik: Yeah, Jesus, God, Krishna—all of us.

Me: Wow, that's one helluva party!

Erik: Maybe we get around to playing poker. But seriously, the conversations you have with God aren't like a telephone call, where you know what you're dialing and you know the voice you're going to hear in return. When you connect to the pure Source of energy, It communicates with you in a way that you understand. It can change and morph into anything It needs to be to place you in a comfort zone so that you can feel at peace with It. So, when you connect with God and you have conversations with God, one day you might need that strong God—the one that just tells you "yes" or "no." And then some days, you need the God that just wants to sing to you, cuddle you—I don't know, just be with you.

Me: Does that have something to do with matching vibrational frequencies? Is there physics behind how God changes? I mean, if you have one of those days where you think you need to be nudged to go on the right road, does your vibrational energy have anything to do with how—

Erik: Yeah. When you change your emotional status, that changes your thoughts, your vibrational energy.

Me: Uh-huh.

Erik: And when you tune in to the pure Source, if you're— Let's just remember that Pure Energy, or God, is nonjudgmental, so no matter what you come with, that Source is not going to look at you and say, "No, you're not going to understand what I'm going to say, because you're angry, or you're a lower vibration, or you're not seeing it the way I'm seeing it." That never exists. Just delete that whole framework. Whatever you come with—[with any level of] willingness to connect with Pure Source, with God—God will match where you are but not lessen the information.

Me: Oh, okay. Wow.

Erik: Anyway, back to my conversations with God. After I appeared here, once I got my courage up, I did talk with God. I was told that I could choose to be a gift now to the Earth and that I could help many. I actually was in awe. I was told that I always had free will, and I was told how much I was loved. That feeling was unlike anything anyone can ever, ever experience on Earth. I was shown how really great I am—but there's no arrogance or ego. It just *is*. I was humbled at the same time.

Me: Can you tell me more about how God broadcasts to the masses there?

Erik: It usually isn't like a generic message to the masses, like, "Blue-light special on harps, aisle three." Communication is [designed for] each individual being. That's what's so incredible about it.

Me: Wow, so God is some kind of multitasker!

Erik (chuckling): Yeah!

Me: So, what role does God play in our lives as humans?

Erik: When you recognize what I'm telling you, and you believe in the consciousness of God, then your life changes. God watches over the world—watches the consciousness of the whole world—and can destroy it or keep it whole with the snap of a finger. The world itself has a consciousness about it. It's high, high up, and it's accepted by the people on it.

Me: Here's a question from one of the blog members: "I was just reading the blog where Erik was talking about another type of energy beside God. Can you have Erik talk more about this? I thought God was the only energy. These dark beings that Erik talks about, where are they from? A different level? Can Erik talk more about this other energy source other than the God Source. Do these beings need to be shown the Light of God? Do we need to avoid these beings at all costs?"

Erik: Well, apologize to him, 'cause I didn't mean to make it sound like the darker energies were separate or away from God.

[I'm thinking it's pretty cool he picked up on the fact that the member who posed this question was a guy.]

Me: Okay.

Erik: What I meant to express is that they are the *furthest* from God. It doesn't mean that they are separate from God.

Me: Ah! Okay! Just part of the spectrum, then?

Erik: Yeah. Everything is God Source energy. You can't divide away from it.

Me: So, if God is always equated with being love and everything, how can part of that Source energy be evil? Is it evil, really? Would you call it evil, or . . .

Erik: You see, the problem is, when you look at the definition of "evil" made by humans, [you] think that it's so completely separate from God—that it has an identity of its own.

Me: Ah! Okay.

Erik (excitedly): Okay, look. God is the room whether the light's off or the light's on. When the light is off, isn't the room still there?

Me: Yeah. I get it.

Erik: God is the room. It's just different variations of light to darkness. Put it to people that way, Mom; I think they'll get it.

Me: That's very interesting, Erik! Great analogy! You explain things so well.

Erik: Most people like to be in the room with the lights on. Some people love to live in total darkness—but they're still inside the room.

Me: Yeah, and think of the savings in their electric bill! Still, wandering around in darkness might mean stubbing your toe on a sofa or two.

Erik (chuckling): Yeah, right! They see less of the room, hence they think God is not there.

Jamie (to Erik): Aw! That's so— High five on that one, Erik!

Me: Yay! That *was* totally awesome, Erik! I especially like it when you say "hence." That's just so cute.

Erik: Aw, shucks.

Me: Okay. Now, I'm curious about Jesus.

Erik: Jesus was a dude.

Me: Erik! Well, I guess he was.

Jamie (laughing): No, the way he said it, "Jesus was a dude."

Me: Aha! The secret is out!

[Jamie laughs.]

Me: So what was his purpose?

Erik: Imagine— Okay, we're gonna use God, for the lack of a better term.

Me: Okay.

Erik: You know, God pinches off chunks of [Its] own energy, and some of these chunks go into plants [and] insects; to feed the Earth, the soul of the Earth; and some of it goes into people as we are born again into the body. And some stay behind; they don't come to Earth. Those we call either angelic or, you know, holy or pure 'cause they don't taint their energy by choosing to live many different lives on Earth.

Me: Oh, okay. So, those are the angelic beings, celestial beings?

Erik: Yes. And then we have chunks that pull off who have this passion or contract to speak about the Source, the God, the Pure Energy. Jesus was one of many of those types of chunks.

Me: Wow, I never thought I'd hear Jesus being called a chunk.

Erik (chuckling): Yeah, and Buddha, Gandhi, the Dalai Lama, Sai Baba. There are many of these spirits, and I think that's why we get these different religions—because we find someone so comfortable and all-knowing that we want to build a structure around them to understand them more.

Me: Ah, yes!

Erik: That's what humans do—we build structures. We try to measure and compare and contrast and label, and so we did that around Jesus too. Same with Krishna, Buddha, and several others. The point is, they come to Earth, but they don't cycle through life after life after life. And they don't just do it once, either. Jesus has been back. Jesus has been here before. Think about it: Jesus isn't the kinda guy to place judgment and only take those who believe in him and damn the rest!

Me: Oh, no, of course not! So, you're saying that Jesus incarnated here before, more than once?

Erik: Yep.

Me: But I thought you said that these are the souls that don't cycle through over and over again.

Erik: Right. They choose the important or potent times to come back to Earth to be the average person [who helps] people grow. They don't come back hundreds or thousands of times like the regular souls do.

Me: But they remember who they are. They remember that they are part and whole of the God Source, unlike other humans.

Erik: My mama's getting it! So, Jesus truly was the physical son of God, or a part of God.

Me: Aren't we all, though?

Erik: Yes, we are. But again, he was sent to Earth with a consciousness that he was the son of God. We come in without that consciousness. We learn it as we grow, at least some of us do.

Me: So he got the Cliff's Notes! That's not fair!

Jamie (laughing): Yeah, he did!

Me: Did Buddha, Muhammad, and others like them have the same purpose here that Jesus had?

Erik: It would be kinda like Jesus. They're all Masters. Masters who came down to teach.

Me: Erik, have you met saints or gurus, and do you have places of worship there like churches, temples, and so on?

Erik: Yeah, to answer your last question about places of worship, yeah. It's not really a place to go worship, though. It's more of a place to learn and expand. So, it's not so much that, "Sit down and let me lecture to you from this book."

Me: Do you spirits pray to any god or prophet?

[Long pause]

Erik: Well, I guess you could call it prayer, yeah. Yes, we have moments where we can sing and also repeat the same phrases, but it's for *all*. It's not for the one God; it's for all of us.

Me: Yeah, that makes sense, because we're all an inseparable collective anyway.

Erik: Yes.

Me: If we worship some other entity, we're really worshipping ourselves.

Erik: Yeah, you got it, Mom.

That was all Erik was able to share about religious subject matter during this session that immediately followed his death. But given his recent passing, I was—and am—impressed with his insight and how it seems to agree so closely with the recent perspective of many quantum physicists. Some scientists believe God is a massive field of consciousness, and that we are both a part and the whole of that field. Erik describes our relationship with God as a hologram. For instance, let's say a picture of Erik represents his soul or consciousness. God is a massive picture of Erik (as It is with all of us) and each pixel in that massive "God image" of Erik is a tiny individual picture of Erik.

Many organized religions teach that a deity created us in its image, so this does make a certain kind of sense. Perhaps God is a collective consciousness of all of our souls—the Supreme Energy Source—and perhaps we are not only that whole, but also the part of that consciousness that behaves like an arm, reaching out to explore and evolve. As we travel to the earthly plane and become incarnate, we use that plane as a laboratory where we utilize struggles, adversities, human emotions, and other factors to evolve toward some end goal—perhaps to become love itself.

Einstein tried to define love in terms of mathematical equations, so perhaps he also understood that love is some form of energy toward which all consciousness evolves. I find this comforting, because not only are we connected to a higher universal consciousness, we are connected to each other, independent of time, independent of space, independent of dimension. That said, I am as close to Erik now as I ever was before.

15

WHO ARE WE, AND WHY ARE WE HERE?

The human experience can be, well, Hell on Earth sometimes, can't it? My next few questions for Erik echo my penchant for understanding the underpinnings of life as a human being. Who are we? Why are we here? How do we operate? What makes us tick? So, I plow ahead with the not-so-subtle start:

The Nature of Us

Me: Erik, what are we, really?

Erik: We're part of a big field of energy—of consciousness made of energy. We're individual segments of that consciousness, but we're also the whole—kind of like a hologram—which can be both the whole and parts of the whole at the same time. In the simplest of sentences, we are sentient energy.

[He shared these insights before, but they are a welcomed refresher.]

Me: What is our purpose as parts and as the whole of that field of consciousness?

Erik: We try to seek lower entropy, both as separate units and as part of the whole. We project to the whole what we do individually. We are here to evolve to a higher level.

Me: So what is that, actually? I know lower entropy means lower disorder or chaos, but what does that mean in practical terms? What's the endpoint?

Erik: For one thing, we try to get to the point where we stay in Heaven to work with others who are still on the earthly plane, striving to evolve themselves.

Me: Okay, I can see that as the endpoint for us as individual souls, but what about the whole? What's our goal as the entire field of consciousness, as all the souls put together?

Erik: We seek to become love—unconditional love—as individuals and for the universe as a whole, for each soul to embrace. That's the lowest entropy. That's the endpoint.

[Wow, that's going to take some time to digest. I find this whole love equals energy thing fascinating, because when I love someone unconditionally, I feel this strange vibration, a sense that my soul is expanding beyond all limits. It feels electrifying and invigorating, like I'm plugged into some huge, benevolent energy source.]

Me: I've heard someone describe us as consciousness moving through various perspectives experiencing ourselves.

Erik: Damn! Who wrote that?

Me: I don't remember.

Erik: Yeah, Mom, that's who we are. That pretty much nailed it.

Me: So, Erik, why are problems so much more difficult to deal with in the afterlife? Why is it preferable to deal with them here? I ask this to help those who are considering suicide to realize that their problems not only stay with them when they cross over, but they also are much more difficult to manage.

Erik: Mom, we deal with issues on the earthly plane, not in Heaven. So, if you don't get something done in your earthly lifetime, then you're gonna have to deal with it when you reincarnate.

Me: Oh, all right. But in your case—

Erik: Wait, I'm not finished. If we leave a lot of [earthly] things undone, and we come back to the afterlife, we can be remorseful; we can be very disappointed and unhappy with ourselves, but we're not able to start working on things again until we go back to the earthly plane.

Me: Why is that?

Erik: Because of the duality, Mom. In the afterlife, everyone acts at the full level of their enlightenment. Souls here are very helpful to each other: very loving, nurturing, and wanting to be of service to one another. It's there on the earthly plane that we forget who we are, where we've been, and what we're supposed to be doing. That's spiritual amnesia. So we get [on Earth], and we don't remember who and what we are and what our spiritual blueprint is; and when we get to the earthly plane, we usually start working on those issues right away. Those issues make life very challenging where you are.

Me: Tell me about it!

Erik: Some people will run toward their issues and get the work done. But most people, when they get adjusted to the earthly plane, start caring about what others think. They seek approval and acceptance; no one wants to be rejected. So what happens is we start giving away pieces of ourselves until we have no clue who in the hell we are and what we're supposed to be doing. It's the struggle to figure out the answers to those questions that supply us with the challenges we need to grow. That rediscovery of ourselves is what we're on the earthly plane to do. It's more about remembering and less about learning.

Me: No pain, no gain—I get it. But Erik, you evolve in the afterlife too, right?

Erik: Yes, but it's mostly about getting therapy and learning new concepts. When I had therapy, I was able to connect the issues I had in my last lifetime to past life events. But when I go back to the earthly plane, I'll get that spiritual amnesia and have to deal with overcoming those issues again. You don't realize it, Mom, but it's a pain to cross over and realize you still have issues to resolve. That's a big deal. You can understand your issues—you can see your issues here in Heaven, from a conceptual perspective—but you need the experiential component to really resolve them and to completely remember who and what you really are. It's like taking organic chemistry; you need to take the lab to totally get it.

Me: Yeah, and even then . . .

[Erik laughs.]

Erik: Okay, imagine you want to know about brownies—fudge brownies—so you read the recipe and you think you got it. Well, you don't. You have to make the brownies, at the risk of burning your fingers in the oven, but then you taste it and you really, really know what a brownie is! Only then can you truly understand the brownie concept.

Me: Oh, great. Now I'm hungry. Well, it sure would be nice if we could just figure out a way to get that experiential component while we're in spirit. I'd like to just have the cue cards instead of being in the play and getting hurt in those action scenes.

Erik: That would be nice, wouldn't it? Yeah, screw all this. Let's just do it here!

Me: Yeah, I vote for that.

Erik: But Mom, you know that's not the point. The whole point of really learning—the purpose—is actually having a place where you can learn. Just think about it: spiritual beings, they don't *learn*—they *remember*. They remember how to access the information and absorb it.

Me: Yeah.

Erik: There's a unity between past, present, and future. There is no struggle or challenge to learn—only a challenge to remember. So, on Earth—bingo! We can erase parts of what we already remembered. We can incarnate on the earthly plane, and we can learn from that struggle between good and bad.

Jamie: Whew! He's talking so fast, I can barely keep up!

Erik: There is some truth to that statement, "You don't know what you have until it's gone."

Me: Yeah, sure!

Erik: When you're in spirit, you can't fucking get away! You can't get away from anything! And frankly, you don't want to get away. That's just who you are. It encompasses you; it feels great. So, it's a little about learning by having respect for where you come from and what you have in the spiritual realm. Also, on Earth, it's a place—

[Pause as Jamie listens.]

Jamie: Oh, this is so cool! I've never heard this before!

[As she conveys what he says, she starts stumbling on the words, giggles, and says, "Oh, my God, I'm stuttering now!" Erik chuckles endearingly.]

Erik: Earth is a place that's a lower dimension, and even though Heaven is multidimensional, there are endless dimensions out there. So, there are other races and, um, you know, groups of people or beings who are in separate dimensional levels that we can't access while we're in spirit.

Me: Really?

Erik: Yeah! But when we reincarnate to Earth, we're incarnating into a fixed dimensional plane. That's why you have people from Earth, the heavens, the stars—we can all be in one place right there on Earth. It's a true mixed community.

Me: Yay, diversity!

Jamie: Ah, I've never really thought of it that way!

Me: Sort of like a gathering place.

Jamie: Yeah, makes me like this place a little more!

Erik: So, we get here and other races of beings are doing the same thing, like, "Oh, let's get together and meet there on Earth! How about Paris, France? We can all be on the same dimension!" And the others go, "Okay. Let's meet up and party."

Me: That's so fascinating! Anything else you wanna add, baby?

Jamie: He says he was messing with the cat.

Me: Yeah, Ringo (one of our family's cats) is at the door again, meowing. I bet cats are easy to mess with.

Erik: Yeah, they're so sensitive to spirits. They're just so much fun to play with.

Me (yelling out): Oh, hush up, Ringo! He's crying. He's just a big baby, a real scaredy cat. Okay, we digressed a little bit.

Erik: Another reason you can't really evolve very much in the afterlife is 'cause you remember how to access the information and absorb it.

That's like a student who has all the answers for a quiz. How can you learn shit that way? You can't.

Me: Yeah.

Erik: And here, there's a unity between past, present, and future, so you don't have that cause and effect that comes from a linear existence. How can you learn from a mistake if you don't have an effect from it? That's like not having any consequences for anything you do.

Me: Interesting. Now, are humans still evolving physically and emotionally? What will we be like thousands of years from now, or tens of thousands of years from now?

Erik: They are evolving emotionally and energetically first, and that's what will cause the physical to change. What will go first are organ systems like the digestive system. We'll still be—I'm going basic here—lung breathers, air breathers. We'll still have hearts, eyes, and senses, but we'll have extrasensory perceptions. And we'll have all of our digits. Um, we'll have more telepathic skills.

Me: Wow.

Erik: We'll eat less because we'll [consume] energy instead of food.

Me: Oh, that's fascinating!

[My friend Robert Burke says he read about a sevemty-seven year-old man who hadn't consumed food or drink for seventy years. He only consumes energy. Apparently they're testing this in a controlled space and he hasn't anything to eat and drink for twenty-eight days.]

Erik: Yeah, I figure a lot of people will like that. But hell, I [still] love me a chocolate cake.

Me: Well, I actually like the idea of still eating a lot, but my thighs don't particularly agree.

Erik: DNA will also be different; it'll be more light-based. That's all I know right now.

Me: It sounds like we're in for some wonderful changes.

As I approach the end of my journey in bringing Erik's and my story to the world, I look back and reflect on how far I've come. I've changed as a person, as a mother, and as a part of a collective fabric that holds us all together. Thanks to Erik, I know who I am in a grander sense, and I have a fuller grasp of how I fit into the bigger picture of the universe and the rules by which it plays. More important, I know why I am here. What mother—what person—can ask for more? I could not have survived this journey without Erik—the boy I brought into this world, whose cuts and bruises I kissed away, whose tears I wiped, whose heart I embraced, whose darkness I tried so hard to fight on his behalf. I couldn't be prouder of who he has become, and of all the good he's brought into the world despite seemingly insurmountable odds.

CLOSING THOUGHTS

I won't pretend that my journey from skepticism to belief has been an easy one. I was terrified of building up false hopes only to have them dashed to pieces. I didn't want to lose Erik twice. And no magical communication from the beyond convinced me overnight. In fact, I was dragged kicking and screaming the entire way, shouting, "This can't be! It goes against everything I've been taught!"

Along with my inner tug-of-war, I had to wage another battle as well: a crusade of wills against other people. Whenever I shared my "Erik encounters" with friends, neighbors, or even strangers, I was often met with confusion, embarrassment, doubt, pity, and criticism. Some would actually appear quite concerned and back away as if they were going to call the mental-health authorities. A few were downright cruel, saying, "Elisa, you have to get over this and move on. These are all just delusions."

On the other hand, I have also encountered many open-minded individuals who are eager to discuss the spiritual matters I am so keen to understand. Some pour out their own stories about visits from their deceased loved ones or their guardian angels, and others are enlivened by sharing their near-death experiences. The wave of relief that so obviously washes over them after voicing these stories tells me that there are a lot of believers out there who are trapped in very dark closets.

With great trepidation, I have also tested the waters in my own career. Occasionally, when appropriate, I have shared my beliefs with patients, and I am surprised by how open most have been. I'm not certain as to why, but perhaps those who need healing are more open to spiritual concepts and conversations. I have also shared my beliefs with a few colleagues, and I was surprised by how many of them reacted positively. Many seemed relieved to have found someone who is both curious and willing to talk about the afterlife, as many physicians report having witnessed deathbed phenomena but such topics remain widely taboo in their professional capacities.

The inner war, the outer war, and my background as a physician with a love for science—these aspects all made my journey a slow and, at times, grueling one. I felt like I was trying to find my way out of a dense forest ablaze with fire. However, fire can either burn one up or steel one's resolve. In my case, my trials strengthened my faith and my belief that there *is* life after death. It also deepened the relationships I have with my family.

Before Erik's death, I frankly had no idea what my family's beliefs were about life after death. It just never came up. In fact, as a collective, our family didn't really have any strong beliefs about anything other than the importance of integrity, work ethic, compassion, love, and other similar values. Since then, Erik has carried us all through this journey together, broadening our understanding of such things and binding us in a wider belief system that transcends this life and this three-dimensional plane in which we live. My relationship with Erik has also changed. We've always been close, and I miss the times when we hung out in his truck, listening to Lil Wayne or just fielding the questions he had about being a teenager. As a doctor and a mother, part of me wanted to "fix" his struggle with depression, and God knows I tried to help in the ways that I knew how. But that's not what a relationship should be about.

Now, Erik and I have a richer relationship. We talk more and about a larger range of subjects than we ever did before—and we do so as equals. We laugh together; we cry together; we chill together. No one is trying to fix anyone. But I'm still his mother, and he knows that. And I'm blessed with what every mother ultimately dreams of: to have a child who is happy, fulfilled, and engaged in a life's work that brings great joy.

Is there sufficient proof for immortality and the existence of the afterlife? No, not 100 percent. For me, there never will be until I am there, and that's okay. Being an open-minded skeptic is healthy. It's the closed-minded skeptic who keeps humanity at a standstill. If the closed-minded among us had their way, we'd still think the Earth was flat and at the center of our solar system. In the end, it's all about a mix of science and faith. How much of each is up to you.

Not only am I no longer a closed-minded skeptic, but I also have a different understanding about relationships: I know now that they don't have to end at death. When our loved ones die, they only shed their bodies like a suit of clothes. They still have their memories, their emotions, and their love. In fact, their perspective on these matters is even clearer *after* death. They see us for who and what we truly are: human beings who are doing the best we can to remember and become who we are—the embodiment of unconditional love. They remember that struggle all too well. And with the new perspectives gained from their passing, their relationship with us becomes richer, deeper, and even more loving.

I also learned that not only can we still communicate with our loved ones but they want us to. They don't want to be forgotten. They don't want us to "get over" their death and "move on." When it comes to love, death is no match.

Erik and I hope that you've enjoyed reading about this journey that we've traveled together. Knowing that life doesn't end after death—that death is just like walking through a gossamer veil—can provide a great deal of comfort. Although life can be filled with hardships, challenges, and tragedies, in each struggle lies a beautiful lesson you can embrace for spiritual growth. Sometimes, you have to eat a lot of oysters before you find that pearl.

If you'd like to accompany us further in this adventure-laden (and sometimes pothole-riddled) journey through death, the survival of consciousness, and the nature of the afterlife, please join the conversation at channelingerik.com. Since its inception, the *Channeling Erik* blog has blossomed into an enormous community of both teachers and students who, with Erik's irreverent guidance, travel that spiritual path together. And we'll continue to search for answers, probably discovering even more questions as we go.

ACKNOWLEDGMENTS

I offer my heartfelt gratitude to my husband, Rune; to my children Kristina Braly, Michelle Watts and her husband, Shane, Lukas Medhus, and Annika Medhus; my parents José and Jacqueline; and to my sister, Laura White, and her husband, Jim, for being a part of this collective journey from grief to comfort, and from mystery to understanding. Because of you, we have all never been closer—something rarely seen in families who have lost a child.

I'd like to thank Kim O'Neill for helping me make the first contact with Erik, which I so desperately needed. Kim, your gifts never cease to amaze me.

Jamie, you're something special, and the chemistry you have with my son is both touching and entertaining. I'm glad he has you as his friend, regardless of the pest that he can be. And what can I say about your gift? I couldn't ask for a better voice for my son. You have given him life. For that, I am grateful.

I'd also like to acknowledge my literary agent, Rita Rosenkranz, and the editor in chief at Beyond Words Publishing, Cynthia Black, both of whom believed in my work—and in me—when others did not. To believe in this book is to believe in my son, and that faith gives meaning to his death.

To managing editor Lindsay S. Brown, copy editor Sheila Ashdown, and proofreader Jennifer Weaver-Neist, I thank you for your patience. It must be difficult dealing with a greenhorn who is a bit broken.

To designer Devon Smith, I'm grateful for the artful beauty you bring to the book—truly brilliant. And these acknowledgements would not be complete without giving my sincerest gratitude to those who give my book a voice that is worthy of the public's ear: Kim Dower, publicist extraordinaire, along with the marketing and publicity team at Beyond Words: Whitney Quon, Leah Brown, and Jackie Hooper.

Finally, I give thanks to my editors, Sylvia Spratt and Emily Han, for finding a diamond in the rough and working tirelessly to etch it out. I'm grateful for all you've taught me.

Erik, my son, I am so proud of what you have become and of how your noble cause is changing the lives of so many. You're opening eyes and hearts, and you're doing so in a way that is playful and authentic. What's more, you're fulfilled and happy. No mother could ask for more. I love you.

No one lives in a vacuum. No on sits idly on an island waiting for a passing ship to bring them back into the folds of humanity. This book is the product of a team rich in dedication and faith forged by integrity and passion. Jamie, Erik, and I couldn't be prouder to be a small piece of that grand puzzle.

NOTES

1. Thomas Campbell, *My Big TOE: The Complete Trilogy* (Huntsville, AL: Lightning Strikes Books, 2007), 118.

2. It's not certain whether this quotation actually originated with Arthur Schopenhauer, though it has been attributed to him since the 1950s. In any case, whoever is the author, it's a powerful message.

3. Doreen Virtue, *The Lightworker's Way: Awakening Your Spiritual Power to Know and Heal* (Carlsbad, CA: Hay House, 1997).

4. Nassim Haramein, "What Is the Origin of Spin?" The Resonance Project (2004): theresonanceproject.org/pdf/origin_of_spin.pdf.

5. Max Born and Albert Einstein, Letter from Albert Einstein to Max Born, March 3, 1947, *The Born–Einstein Letters: Correspondence between Albert Einstein and Max and Hedwig Born from 1916 to 1955* (New York: Macmillan, 1971), 158.

6. Haramein, "What Is the Origin of Spin?"

DISCUSSION AND READING GROUP QUESTIONS

1. Before reading the book, what were your thoughts or beliefs regarding the afterlife? Were you a believer? A skeptic?

2. If you are skeptical of an afterlife, what do you find most challenging about it?

3. If you believe in an afterlife, what could you say to a skeptic that might convince him or her?

4. Have you had a near-death experience, or know of anyone who has? If so, what was your reaction? How did it affect or change you?

5. Can you think of a time in your life when you may have received a communication from a loved one who is on the other side?

6. What are your thoughts about Jamie's role as a "spirit translator"?

7. How do you connect/relate to Elisa's story and experience?

8. What has your experience been after losing a loved one? How did you deal with loss? How does it compare to Elisa's journey through grief?

9. What are your thoughts about Erik's pranks and messages, as described in part 1?

10. What are your thoughts about Erik's description of the afterlife, in chapter 8?

11. Do you fear death? Has that fear abated or eased after reading this book?

12. After reading the book, how have your ideas or beliefs in the afterlife changed? Have they stayed the same? Are you still a skeptic or a believer?

13. After reading the book, do you feel inspired to learn how to communicate with your deceased loved one(s)?

14. Have you read any other books on the same subject matter? If so, how does this book differ?